Flashlight

Women Pastors, Same-Gender
Relationships, God's Flashlight

Benjamin L. Yancey

No Part of this book may be produced, stored in a retrieval system, or transmitted by any means without the written permission of the author.

© 2023 Benjamin L. Yancey. All rights reserved.

ISBN: 978-1-961392-81-6

Dedication

I dedicate this book to my late parents. My Father, Pastor Emeritus Reverend William C Yancey Sr, and my Mother, Adeline V. Yancey. Words cannot express the gratitude and love I have for their support throughout my life. Their love for me directed and guided me to come to know the Lord Jesus Christ for myself and accept him as my savior.

I also dedicate this book to my beautiful, loving wife, Norma J. Yancey, who has been by my side every step of the way. She has been a constant inspiration for me. Whether I have a singing engagement or a preaching engagement, she is always there to support me. I also thank God for my Children Kenesha, Shayla, and Lonnie, who truly are a gift from God. I also thank God for my loving family, Five Brothers, and Three Sisters. We support each other and are always there for one another.

CONTENTS

Dedication iii
About the Author vi
Preface ix
Chapter 1: Introduction 1
   Light into Sin 1
   Light into Society 3
   The Light of Truth 6
   Light of the Constitution 9
   Light into Today's Darkness 12
   Light into Division 15
Chapter 2: Pastoring 20
   Light into Who God is 20
   Light into Pastoring 26
   Light into The Controversy? 29
Chapter 3: Women Pastors 35
   Light into: Is it Biblical? 35
   Light into Biblical Facts 44
   Light into God's Word 50
Chapter 4: Male and Female 53
   Light of Creation 53
   Light Into God Makes No Mistake 56

Chapter 5: Same-Gender Relationships 60
    Light Into Same-Gender Relationships 60
    Light into The Lie 63
    Light into the Debate 65
    Light Into Marriage Created By God 69
    Light Into The Answer God's Solution 74

Chapter 6: God's Flashlight 77
    Flashlight: Let our light shine. 77
    Flashlight into The Remedy 79

Chapter 7: Sins 84
    Various Sins 84
    Scripture References: 87

About the Author

Pastor Rev. Benjamin L. Yancey accepted his Called into the Gospel Ministry in 1997 under the Leadership of his Father the late Pastor William C. Yancey Sr. at Leadership M. B. Church. He became the host of Leadership's Radio ministry in 1998. During his time at Leadership M. B. Church, and served as President of the Mission Society, President of Pastor's Aide, President of Men's Ministry, and President of Music Ministry. He also served as Youth Minister and Adult Sunday School Teacher.

Pastor Benjamin L. Yancey served as Associate Minister at Leadership M. B. Church from 1997 thru 2005. He left to assist another Pastor in the city at Genesis M. B. Church from 2005 to 2007. God called Pastor Benjamin L. Yancey to organize Exodus Baptist Church in 2007. In 2015 Exodus Baptist Church Merged with New Paradise M. B. Church. After the merger, the name was changed to New Paradise United Baptist Church of Milwaukee, WI. God has truly been a blessing to this ministry through Pastor Benjamin L. Yancey.

Rev. Benjamin L. Yancey is also a member of The Yancey Brother's Music Ministry in Milwaukee, WI. They and the Yancey Family have recorded Various songs, including "He's Right There." Pastor Benjamin L. Yancey is married to the love of his life, First Lady Norma J. Yancey. They have (2) beautiful Daughters, Kenesha and Shayla, and (1) son Lonnie. Pastor Benjamin L. Yancey's greatest desire is to change people's lives by Preaching the book that God wrote.

Preface

I am a Pastor of a local Church in Milwaukee, Wisconsin. Born and raised in Milwaukee. I have eight siblings Five Brothers and Three Sisters. We grew up as Children of a Preacher. My Father also Pastored in this City for over 50 years. I know that the word of God says, "none is perfect but the Father which is in Heaven," but my mother was as close to perfect as one can get. We were truly a united family when I say united, I mean we did everything together.

We went to the Grocery store together; we went fishing together, and we also went to Church together. We went everywhere together. I truly thank God for my family. Although my parents are gone on, they did a job well. I enjoyed our yearly family trips going to Memphis Tennessee. Our trips to the South were breathtaking. Visiting our Granddad's farm, we did not know anything about farming, so all of this was new to me and my siblings.

Southern life was different than what we knew growing up in Milwaukee. Our visits each year helped us to see and appreciate the things that we had. I remember the first time we had to go to the bathroom and our cousin was going to take us to the bathroom. He told us to follow him and the next thing we knew; we were going outside of the house. After walking for a while, my eldest brother asked our cousin where we were going. This was our introduction to what they called an outhouse.

That had to be one of the worst of our experiences in the south. I also remember when our grandfather asked us to go down yonder to get something for him, we went outside and stood on the porch and when our mother came outside, she asked us what we were doing. She wanted to know why we had not left to get what our grandfather told us to get. Looking at each other with confused looks on our faces, we asked our mother "where is yonder? My experiences with my relative in the south will always have lasting fond memories.

We learned a great deal about the south how to make homemade ice cream, plow fields, feed hogs, and southern hospitality. One thing I do want to say about the south in the late sixties and early seventies' visiting our granddad's farm. Living in the north a person does not know darkness until you went down south. There were no streetlights out in the country, someone could be standing next to you, and you could not see them. Growing up as a (PK) Preacher's kid, we did not have a lot but what we did have we appreciated.

We never went to bed hungry; we did not have the best of anything, yet we lacked nothing. Three things were Constance's in our life, Church, School, and Chores. One of my brothers once said we went from the delivery room at the Hospital to the Church. I truly thank God for my parents bringing me up in a spiritual home. There was no secular music in our home, we did not need birthday parties there were nine of us. We made up our games to play. Sometimes I ask myself why God blessed my family with so many talents. Everyone in my family sings or plays an instrument.

Even most of our children sing and play instruments. As I got older, I begin to do crazy things. But no matter what I found myself getting into because of my upbringing, I always found myself drawn back to my roots. Regardless of who we are none of us are free from making bad choices in our lives. I often hear people say that if they could live their lives over again that they would do things differently.

I would like to say that if I could do it all over again, I would not change a thing. Everything that I have done and everything that I had to go through has helped to shape me to be the Man that I am today. Think about it if you could change only one thing, that one thing would erase many people and events in your life. In all things give thanks, just be thankful.

I thank God for blessing me with my Children, Two Beautiful Daughters Kenesha and Shayla, and a Handsome son Lonnie. I most certainly thank God for the Gift of my Beautiful Wife Norma J. Yancey who is the love of my life. I often tell people that I did not choose to marry my wife. I say that because I do not want to take the credit I choose someone so beautiful when in fact she was a blessing from God. I give God all the Glory for everything that has happened in my life whether Good or Bad. Because I do believe what God has for me, it is for me.

Chapter 1: Introduction

Light into Sin

I would like to shine a flashlight into why I chose these topics to write about. Sin is Sin, but still there lies a difference in Sin. We know that all transgression is Sin. Sin Is "any want of conformity unto or transgression of the law of God" in the inward state and habit of the soul, as well as in the outward conduct of life, whether by omission or commission. The moral character of a man's actions is decided by the moral state of his heart.

The disposition to sin, or the habit of the soul that leads to the sinful act, is itself also sin. Adam's sin consisted of his yielding to the assaults of temptation and eating the forbidden fruit. It involved in it, the sin of unbelief, virtually making God a liar, and the guilt of disobedience to a positive command. Nevertheless, there is still a difference between **Sinning and living in Sin**. Everyone can repent for their Sins. Jesus tells us that we must repent of our sins.

But how can one repent for a sin when they are deliberately living in that sin? Jesus says in his word whatever you are doing when I return keep doing it. Christ also says that he came to set us free from our sins.

When discussing Same-gender relationships and LGBTQ, I would like everyone to know that those who choose to live under this banner have a God-given right (Free Will) and a Governmental right (The Constitution) to live how they choose.

As Apostle Paul wrote to the church in Rome he said, "My prayer to God for Israel is that they might be saved." This is my prayer also that those who have chosen to live this lifestyle examine the light of the words in this book to understand that they have willfully decided to live contrary to their natural God-created design. There is no Sin that we can commit that does not offer forgiveness except Blasphemy. The problem is we cannot ask God for forgiveness for sins that we know we are going to continue doing.

We cannot tempt God to forgive us for knowingly doing wrong, or expect God to forgive us because He is God. God hates sin. What shall we say then? Shall we continue in sin, that grace may abound? God forbid. How shall we? If sin has been the occasion of grace and favor, ought we not to continue in it? Whosoever committeth sin transgresseth also the law: for sin is the transgression of the law. And we know that Christ came to take away our sins; and in him is no sin.

Whosoever abideth in him sinneth not: whosoever sinneth hath not seen him, neither known him. And He that keepeth his commandments dwelleth in Him, and He in Him. And hereby we know that he abideth in us, by the Spirit which He hath given us. For this is good and acceptable in the sight of God our Saviour, who will have all be saved, and to come unto the knowledge of the truth. That is, it is good to God that we should pray for all. The reason is that He wants their salvation, and it is agreeable to him that we should pray for it. Who will have all men be saved? That is, it is by his nature, his feelings, and his desires.

Light into Society

<u>Ye are the light of the world</u>. It is not easy to be a dedicated Christian. Our society is not a friend to God or God's people. Whether we like it or not, there is a conflict between us and the world. Why? Because we are different from the world, and we have different attitudes. God is counting on us as believers to be a leading light for people whose lost in this dark and sinful world. Light is the emblem of happiness, knowledge, and holiness. Let your light so shine before men, that they may see your good works, and glorify your Father which is in heaven.

It is not sufficient to have light we must walk in the light, and by the light. Our whole conduct should be a perpetual comment on the doctrine we have received, and a constant exemplification of its power and truth. These issues have not only plagued our society but have also managed to weaken the purpose of the Church and the fabric of our Faith in God. Because of our sin nature, we have once again become lost in the very Garden that God has placed us in.

We have forsaken our natural purpose in pursuit of the very things that look to destroy us physically, mentally, emotionally, and spiritually. If each one of us would take it upon ourselves not to seek what others may think but rather what we think about who we are and why we are here. What is it really that we look for? What is it that drives us to do the things that we do? If we were to be, honest with ourselves, the very thing we seek is the very thing that brings us the most grief in life

Are we driven by the desire of having power, wealth, and riches? We should not seek after the lust of the flesh, the lust of the eyes, and the pride of life. It does not matter how we feel or what we try to do, there will always be those who have less than others. If you are Wealthy, there will always be someone who has more than you. If you feel that you are poor, there will always be someone who has less than you. Regardless of how much or how less someone may have, we are all responsible for the condition in which we live.

We all must take ownership of what is going on in our society today. Every one of us is guilty of the evil and darkness of our society in which we live either by Participation or by our silence in ignoring what we see going on. Either way, we cannot dismiss our obligation toward one another. I can remember the times when we were not only concerned about our Family, but we were also concerned about our neighbors. When I speak of neighbors, I am not just talking about the family next door.

Our neighbors were the families down the street and around the corner. I can remember that if the mother next door were ill, people in the neighborhood would take food to their home to ensure that the family had something to eat. The good thing about this is the family in need did not have to call and ask for help people were willing to help because we were concerned about each other. I remember the time when as a child we did something wrong the neighbors would inform our Parents.

When our parents found out what we had done depending on how bad the act was, we would get a whipping. I told my wife that I got a whipping every other week. She asked me why I got so many whippings; I told her the whippings I received were not for the same thing. Growing up we did not know what we could not do until we did it. Most people today would tell you that you should not whip your children. Most families of color would tell you that it was those whipping that kept us out of jail and away from drugs.

Spare the rod and spoil the child. It did not make us perfect, but it kept us from doing many of the things we see going on in the world today. Now, I am not saying that every child should receive whippings nor am I saying that we received whippings for everything we did wrong. Today people will not say anything when they see children in the neighborhood doing wrong for fear of the children retaliating or even being threatened by the children's parents.

I remember a time when parents let their children go to the neighborhood parks to play without fear of them being shot or never seeing them again. When or how did we become so hateful toward one another? As a people when did we start a war against each other? I have often said to the congregation that there is no thin line between love and hate. There is absolutely nothing between love and hate. We either love or we hate. The truth of the matter is a person does not have to do anything for you to love them, but a person does have to do something to cause you to hate them.

It profits us nothing to hate. Hating someone changes nothing. If I chose to hate you because you are tall, my hate will not cause you to shrink. If I hate, you because you are Black or White it will not change the color of your skin. To be perfectly honest why hate anyone for something that they cannot change anyway. We should love each other because we are all of the Human race.

Question why is it that a thief doesn't want anyone to steal from them? Why is it that a liar doesn't want to be lied to? Why is it that a murderer doesn't want to be killed? We know when we are wrong and what we should not be doing. Life is about choices, and we must choose to do right or wrong.

The Light of Truth

Few problems cause God's people to question His rule more than, "Why do the helpless and the godly suffer and the wicked get away with their crimes?" When it comes to dealing with the injustices in society, the bible teaches us that the righteous have five responsibilities. (1) Truth (2) Praying to the Lord for Justice, (3) Warning the Wicked of Their Danger, (4) Accepting God's Discipline and (5) Collaborating with God for Justice. They that worship God must worship him in Spirit and truth.

To seek the truth, one must ask "what is the truth." The truth is neither Black nor White, it is not a Nationality, it is not an Ethnic background nor is it a religion. The truth also is not Justice nor is it Political. The truth is not based on Wealth, nor is it based on Position. The Truth is also neither male nor female. The truth is not a majority of one. For some people, this means that, in the end, <u>truth doesn't matter</u>. What does it matter whether we can or cannot know what is really "out there"?

If you do what makes you happy and leave others to do the same, what does the truth matter? In this view, if a belief that something is true seems a useful aid to living a contented life, then there is no harm in believing it provided you do not try to make anyone else believe it too. At a more popular level, people tend to treat truth like private property. I have my truth like I have my car. But most importantly, others' truths are dishonored. The only universal truth is that it is always wrong to say someone else's truth is not true.

Within this view, truth is a good thing, even though it is just a social construct. So, what is Truth? Truth is simply Right and wrong. <u>That which is true or by fact or reality.</u> If we are being honest, we must admit that all our lives are marred, one way or another, by deceit and falsehood. We all depart from the truth in our thoughts and actions. If our thoughts are true, it is because they correspond to the world as God made and knows it. If our actions are true, it is because they conform to the way God himself has directed us to live.

Truth should luminate in the hearts and minds of every Man, Woman, Boy, and Girl regardless of the color of our skin, our Character, our religious beliefs, our position, or our wealth. It does not have anything to do with us seeing each other as equals. We will never see one another as equal because we are always looking to find the differences between each other. Notice that when we meet someone for the very first time, we are meeting their representative. We are meeting the person that they would like for us at that time to meet.

There is something wrong with each of us and when we first meet someone, we are not ready for them to meet our flaws. We also know that no one is perfect, so at first sight, we look to find out what and where are their flaws. We will never find, nor will we ever accept the truth until we can see that right is right and wrong is wrong according to the word of God. If you believe something to be right, then it must be right for all. No, an adult and a child cannot be judged by the same truth. If you believe in your heart that it is right for you to pursue your dreams and live and work anywhere, then that same belief must be applied to all people.

How can two separate but equal individuals from diverse backgrounds commit the same crime yet receive two different sentences based on the color of their skin, position in life, or wealth? Why are there some who are advocating segregation and separation? I believe if we would just consider becoming one great congregation in this great nation our country and our individual lives would be much better. Congregation simply means coming together. Can you envision what this world would look like if we all came together? I am not saying that there would not be disagreements, but we should agree to disagree.

Let me add this if each one of us would look upon ourselves as a pencil going through this life what kind of mark would you leave in this world? The first thing we must understand is that the pencil is useless until it is in the hands of someone. This is the key to the legacy in which we leave because whoever is controlling the pencil also controls the marks we will leave in this life. Notice the pencil is relatively unproductive until it has been sharpened. The pencil must be shaved down for that which is on the inside to be effective on the outside. Once this is done it can now be used.

Therefore, whoever is controlling your life as a pencil also determines the marks that you will leave in this world. This is why I love this analogy remember a pencil has two sides. We can use our erasers to erase many of the mistakes that we will make going through this life. You see when we look at it from this perspective when we make mistakes Christ himself erases those bad marks when he tells the father "Father I paid for that mistake." If we live our lives as a pencil for Christ, we would be careful about the marks that we leave.

Light of the Constitution

The Constitution is not a Christian document, but it is a document written by Christians. The concept found in the Constitution of the United States can also be seen in the word of God. Because we have a sinful nature humanity to this day still struggles to shine a light of love, respect, and unity toward everyone. The Constitution was created in 1789 to form a more perfect union. It has been amended 27 times from the eighteenth-century world in which its creators lived.

The first Ten amendments, known collectively as the Bill of Rights, offer specific protections of individual liberty and justice and place restrictions on the powers of government. "The Constitution's first three words **"We the People"** affirm that the government of the United States exists to serve its citizens. The preamble to the Constitution is an introduction to the document. We the People of the United States. The preamble states the purpose of the Constitution and its intentions and laws.

So, as it states "we the people" what people? The definition of people is human beings in general. So, when were individuals of color, not people or not human, and even slaves defined as people? What makes someone a human? A person is a being that has certain capacities or attributes such as reason, morality, consciousness, or self-consciousness, and social relations such as kinship, ownership of property, or legal responsibility. So, when you look at the Constitution you must understand that the writers of the Constitution's minds were blinded by prejudices not to see that people of color were Human beings.

You see for a great period in history it has been said that people of color evolved. To consider that idea one must face this reality. If anyone believes that people of color evolved, then they must admit that people of color are the only race of people that have changed over time. Because the people that they claim evolved are now walking with them, working alone side of them, talking with them, serving in political offices with them, creating their businesses, winning the Nobel Peace prize, served as the President of the United States.

Therefore, The First Amendment (1791) prohibits Congress from obstructing the exercise of certain individual freedoms. In 1963 Dr. King Spoke these words. "In a sense, we have come to our nation's capital to cash a check. When the architects of our Republic wrote the magnificent words of the Constitution and the Declaration of Independence, they were signing a promissory note to which every American was to fall heir. 'This note was a promise that all men, Black men as well as white men would be guaranteed the unalienable rights of life, liberty, and the pursuit of happiness.

But we refuse to believe that the bank of justice is bankrupt. We refuse to believe that there are insufficient funds in the great vaults of opportunity of this nation. So, we have come to cash this check, a check that will give us upon demand the riches of freedom and the security of justice." The late Dr. King dreamed that one day we would have Civil Rights and Equal Rights. Civil rights are not what we believe them to be. If civil rights for Americans were civil, we would not have all these acts. It takes less time for a baby to be born into this world, grow up and become an adult than it took for every human being to be accepted as an equal American citizen.

The **Civil Rights Act (1866)** This **act** declared that all persons born in the United States were now citizens, without regard to race, color, or previous condition. The **Civil Rights Act of 1957**, was the first **civil rights legislation**. The **Civil Rights Act of 1960**. The **Civil Rights Act of 1964**. The **Civil Rights Act of 1968, and** the Fair Housing **Act of 1968**. The **Civil Rights Act of 1991**. If we are to be Civil towards one another, why do we have all these Acts? Power, Greed, and Discrimination toward each other causes division against each other.

    <u>The **pursuit of happiness** is defined as a fundamental right mentioned in the Declaration of Independence to freely pursue joy and live life in a way that makes you **happy**.</u> Freedom of speech, religion, and the press. The right to assemble, bear arms, and due process. These are just some of the first 10 amendments that make up the <u>Bill of Rights</u>. In 1965 Dr. King stated that we as a Black Race needed to gain access to voting so that we would be able to vote for Individuals in Government offices who would do right by the citizens of each state and in Washington D.C.

    So, when Dr. King spoke of equality where did we go wrong? Regardless of race or Nationality elected officials once elected seem to have their agenda which is to stay in office and get what they can for themselves. Despite all the ACT passed, we have managed to find another way to separate, segregate and discriminate against one another. Society may lead us to believe that racism no longer exists but is still judged by the color of our skin, our Character, our religious beliefs, our position, and our wealth.

Light into Today's Darkness

Now, let us look at Society in the 21st century. We must all agree that everything is getting worse instead of better. Not too long ago a Profession Football player of color chooses to stand up against police brutality only to find himself standing alone. He never did anything wrong he did what our Constitution grants us the liberty to do. He had not committed any crime against society, he had not committed any injustice against the brave and heroic members of our military and those that served this great country.

What he did was he chose to kneel at the singing of the National Anthem. The United States national anthem was first recognized by law in 1931, there was no prescription as to behavior during its playing. On June 22, 1942, the law was revised indicating that those in uniform should salute during its playing, while others should simply stand at attention, men removing their hats. Our Military has fought and continues to fight so that we the people of the United States would have a voice.

Now, let me be noticeably clear our military is the Greatest example of unity. I say this because our military is not RACIST. Various people from ethnic backgrounds make up our military. Who may at times be accused of discriminating against someone, but the military is not racist because they fight to defend All Americans. The American flag. The stripes represent the original 13 Colonies, and the stars represent the fifty states of the Union. The colors of the flag are symbolic as well; red symbolizes hardiness and valor, white symbolizes purity and innocence, and blue represents vigilance, perseverance, and justice.

So, where is the Justice for all Americans, everyone knows the hardness that the people of color had to endure even to be where we are today. Also, why is the American flag important? The flag has been used to display our nationalism, as well as our rebellion, and everything else in between. The flag is so important that its history tells the story of America itself. It represents the freedom, dignity, and true meaning of being an American.

If these statements are true and they are, then what did he do, or how did he bring disgrace to the Military or even to the flag? Where is our voice? We should always love one another and learn how to agree to disagree without hate or violence. We should see that to effect change. We must learn how to come together. Dr. King wanted all people to have the right to vote where their voices would be heard through their vote. For the people in America, the only true way our voices can be heard is through our voting on the issues we face.

When we cast our votes, they are now counted, and the number of votes now weighs in the balance and the outcome of the Issue voted on. This system should illustrate to us that change can only come by way of us coming together and taking a stand on what we believe. We cannot continue to expect anything to change when we as individuals refuse to stand together on issues that continue to plague our society. This statement "Together we Stand and Divided We Fall" has never been truer than in the society we now live in.

There also was another prominent sports figure who stated nationally that his mother was wrong for whipping him as a child. Although coming from humble beginnings and now living a life of being well-off. If he truly would take a step back and realize that if it had not been for his upbringing, and the discipline he received from his mother he would have never made it to the NFL. He would not even be the Man he is today. We must never forget that everything we go through in life helps to shape and mold us into who we are today.

I am not saying that everyone should receive whippings. There are times when punishments work. There is one thing that I would agree with them on and that is Time outs. Parents needed to take Time Out to discipline their children. Everything that has and will happen to us whether we deem them good or bad helps to mold us into whom we will eventually become.

Anyone who is not ashamed of speaking the truth must admit that since parents stop disciplining their children the world has become worst. Never before have we seen so many of our youth out of control in the streets of our cities. We have so many shootings at schools, malls, theaters, night clubs. We as parents must accept some responsibility for the behavior of our children. God blessed us with our children to raise them to be the best that they can be. Let us stand up together and help our youth be their best in this society.

Light into Division

We, as a people of color, have come from being slaves in a cotton field to being slaves on other fields and in other fields. Not to offend anyone with these words. What does it mean to be a Slave? To serve as a slave, submitting one's own will to his master. When you are unable to speak the truth because of who employs you, then you are enslaved to that company, individual, or BRAND. Throughout society, many of us hold positions of authority. Far too often, we forget that with authority comes great responsibility.

To whom much is given, much is required. When we know that something is wrong and refuse to say anything we become partakers of that wrong. When we forget to fulfill our responsibility, we usually abuse the power of our position. And when power is abused, we become selfish and unconcerned about others. God has called every believer to be a good and faithful steward. To be a good and faithful steward we must acknowledge that God Himself is the owner of all things.

We must act like managers, not owners, we must seek the best for God and others, not for ourselves. We must think about the possible consequences before we act, we must keep an open heart for communication not a clenched fist for retaliation, and we must minister to others as Jesus would and not as our fallen natures desire of us. Many people who have been blessed to make it out of their impoverished upbringing whether through sports or entertainment choose to sit silently.

Nothing will ever change until we as a people can come together and stand together for Truth. The Bus boycott would have never changed a thing if they did not work together. Even in the religious community we sit silently and watch this world, this Nation, our country, our States, and our cities become increasingly corrupted, and we can't come together to speak the truth. One should ask themselves, why was prayer taken out of our Public Schools?

The answer is simple we sat by and did nothing. Oh, but some would say that we fought to keep prayer in our Schools. I disagree because if we were committed to keeping prayer in our schools all we needed to do was come together and pray. Prayers of the righteous availeth much, but even we as believers can't come together for a common goal. It will always remain difficult for us as a nation to come together when the top leaders of our Country can't seem to come together on anything.

If we as a people are fighting in the White House, The Senate, The House of Representatives, and our local government, where can one look for unity? Until we can find a way to set aside our differences and learn how to agree to disagree, we will always be divided against one another. But this sounds confusing since we are known as THE UNITED STATES OF AMERICA. Where is the UNITY? A House divided cannot stand. Why are there Poor People, Low-income people, Middle- class people, and Rich people?

How difficult is it for us to just be people? We are all people, some of whom just need more help than others. How is it that the People who have the least must pay the most in interest just to acquire anything? How is it that Banks would rather foreclose on a Family's home and kick them out instead of reducing their Monthly payment to a payment that they can pay? This way the families can stay in their homes and the Banks can still receive their money over time.

No, they kick the Families out and let the house sit in the neighborhoods and become an eyesore for that neighborhood. Wisconsin is a Marital State. This means that a creditor can go after your spouse for your unpaid debt. For example: if your wife has unpaid medical bills the bill collectors can come after you to pay her bills. Well, if this is a Marital State, and since the creditors can come after me for a medical bill belonging to my wife, then why can't my insurance pay the portion of her medical bill that her insurance doesn't cover?

The benefits of being a Marital State should benefit both ways not just for the Companies. Why is it that the Wealthy who can pay top dollar pay the least in interest? Could it be so the rich stay rich, and the poor stay poor? Life's struggles are real, and it does not matter what a person's color or Ethnic background is. When we look at crime in America, we must ask ourselves what is going on. Some crimes are being committed in broad daylight that once only happened in darkness. There was a time when everyone cared for each other.

If someone saw you doing something wrong, they would stop you and tell your Parents. But today, people refuse to say anything because of fear that the Child would curse them out or that the Parents might try and harm them. Why did we choose to give up on one another? When did we stop caring for each other? What has caused us to look the other way? What has caused us to develop an attitude that if it is not me, it is not my problem.? Are we still our brother's keeper?

We, as individuals, can only answer that question. We live in a society today where people do not care how they look, how they dress, how they carry themselves, and how they speak to each other. Do you remember when People respected themselves and also had respect for others? One thing is for sure we have been able to elect people of color into political offices throughout this Nation. We have, by the grace of God, had an opportunity to elect a President of color who served this Country well for not one but two terms in office.

Dr. King declined to serve in the White House in any capacity to stay true to his beliefs and his calling to unite Americans as a People. His dream has since become a Nightmare. When you look at how some People of Color who are serving in Political positions from City Counsel to the Senate have changed their agenda now that they are in those Positions, they vote on every issue that weighs in the balance of the future of all Americans.

They vote on issues of minimum wages, tax issues, Health Care, and other American concerns. They are willing to Cut Programs for Youth, cut Health care for Seniors and Low-income families to try, as they say, to balance the Budget or cut spending. You never hear them voting on reducing their pay when they sit in a room and do nothing but play with the Future of American lives.

There are two truths that we need to uncover, and that is the true Enemy and Justice. Justice is the morally fair and right state of everything. To have justice as a person's character trait means that they are just and treat everyone the same, or how they would like to be treated. From a scriptural point of view, justice means loving our neighbor as we love ourselves and is rooted in the character and nature of God.

As God is just and loving, so we are called to do justice and live in love. Jesus said unto him, thou shalt love the Lord thy God with all thy heart, and with all thy soul, and with all thy mind. This is the first and great commandment. And the second is like unto it. Thou shalt love thy neighbor as thyself. Therefore, justice must be shown out of love, for without love, it JUST**-IS.**

Here lies this great truth. The truth is that Mankind is his Enemy. To understand this simple truth, one must be able to identify the adversary. An adversary is an enemy or someone who opposes someone else. An adversary is related to the word adverse, meaning "against or contrary." Therefore, where is this great Adversary or enemy? The best way to find this enemy is to look **IN-A-ME**.

A good man out of the good treasure of his heart bringeth forth that which is good, and an evil man out of the evil treasure of his heart bringeth forth that which is evil. What have we done to one another that we view each other as Adversaries? Why do we assume someone is out to get us? Before I begin with the topics, I want to shed a pinpoint light on why there seems to be a debate about such issues.

The reason there seems to be a debate is that most, if not all, of the information written on these subjects that I have discovered during my research, is ridiculously false. We are all entitled to our own opinion, but where are we searching to find this information that leads to various opinions? What sources do we rely on to come to our conclusions? One must admit the Constitution was written from Biblical references.

Many of our Laws were written from Biblical references. Now I am not trying to be disrespectful to anyone, nor am I trying to belittle anyone. There is no way any one of us can speak about God as if he were Human. The problem lies when a man thinks he can debate with God. To fully understand what I am trying to help each one of us realizes, I would like to suggest that you read the 38th Chapter of Job. But first, let us examine something.

Chapter 2: Pastoring

Light into Who God is

It saddens me to say many people do not know who God is. Many people who regularly attend worship services do not know who God is. God is not who we think him to be, nor is he whom we want him to be. God is God all by himself. So, let me start by saying that no Human can say who God is. For us to even begin to try and understand who God is, we must return to the beginning of the book of Genesis. Genesis chapter one is where it all begins.

Listen; it states in the beginning, God created the Heavens and the Earth. So, think about this, it is not the beginning of creation, it is not the beginning of Humanity, and it is most certainly not the beginning of God. So, what is it the beginning of? It is the beginning of Time and the beginning of the introduction of God himself. It is the beginning of time so that we may be able to understand things and events that have taken place in the past, present, and future.

In this beginning, God is introducing himself to us and his creation. Notice how he tells us in chapter one about creation and then breaks it down precisely how creation came about in chapter Two. Without the word of God, we would not even know how God separated the darkness from the light. We would not know that the light would be called day and the darkness would be called night. God introduces himself and calls time to begin to record all events thereafter.

Before the creation mentioned in chapter 1, all was ETERNITY. Time signifies duration measured by the history of events: but before the creation, there could be no measurement of duration, and consequently no time; therefore, in the beginning, it must necessarily mean the commencement of time which followed and everything produced by God's creative acts. As we begin to try and form an opinion on these subjects, let us reframe from playing word games and distorting the meanings of God's word.

It is not a mark of wisdom to try to second-guess God because His ways and thoughts are far beyond our comprehension. We make God after our image and believe He thinks and acts just as we do, and we are wrong! God is God. What or who is a God? In monotheistic thought, God is a supreme being, creator deity, and principal object of faith. God is conceived as being omniscient (all-knowing), omnipotent (all-powerful), omnipresent (all-present), and having an eternal and necessary existence.

OMNIPOTENCE which theology ascribes to God. Scripture affirms that all power belongs to God, that all things are possible for God, and that God's power exceeds what humans can ask or think. In Scripture, God's omnipotence is not a matter of abstract speculation but a force to recognize. God's power is revealed in God's creating and sustaining of the universe, in the incarnation, in Christ's death on the cross, and in the ongoing ministry of the church.

OMNIPRESENCE Being present everywhere at once. Because God created the heavens and the earth, He is present in the whole of creation and its parts. King David realized that there was nowhere he could go to escape God's presence, and no conditions, such as darkness, could hide him from God. Even though God is present everywhere, He is not visible everywhere. He can be fully present and yet hidden from the eyes of humanity.

OMNISCIENCE State of being all-knowing. Scripture affirms God's immeasurable understanding; God's omniscience is not a matter of speculation. God's knowledge is a matter of personal experience. God knows us intimately. Such knowledge is cause for alarm for the unrighteous but confident for God's saints. God in Christianity is the eternal being who created and preserved all things.

Christians believe God to be both transcendent (wholly independent of and removed from the material universe) and immanent (involved in the world). God is not merely one of a plethora of gods from which we may select to worship. He is the omnipotent Creator and Redeemer of mankind. What was happening before God spoke the universe into existence? That may seem like an impractical hypothetical question, but it is not.

God doesn't act arbitrarily, and the fact that He created something suggests that He must have had some magnificent purposes in mind. What, then, **God existed in sublime glory**? God is eternal; He has neither a beginning nor an end. Therefore, He is self-sufficient and needs nothing more than Himself to exist or to act. "God has a voluntary relation to everything He has made, but He has no necessary relation to anything outside of Himself."

God needs nothing, neither the material universe nor humans, and yet He created both. If you want something to boggle your mind, meditate on the concept of the eternal, that which has neither beginning nor end. As creatures of time, you and I can easily focus on the transient things around us; but it is difficult, if not impossible, to conceive of that which is eternal. Contemplating the nature and character of the Triune God, who always was, always is, and always will be, and who never changes, is a task that overwhelms us.

"In the beginning, God." If God is God, as we understand the word, He is eternal and needs nothing; He is all-knowing, all-powerful, and everywhere present. To have a "limited god," you must first redefine the very word "God" because, by the very definition, God has no limit. Furthermore, if God is limited and "getting greater," then what power is making Him greater? That power would be greater than "God" and therefore be God! And wouldn't that give us two gods instead of one?

But the God of the Bible is eternal and has no beginning. He is infinite and knows no limitations in either time or space. He is perfect and cannot "improve," and is immutable and cannot change. People say that they have Faith in God without truly knowing what faith is. Faith is not, nor has it ever been, believing in what God can do. Faith is and will always be believing in God, period. Someone might believe that God can heal them. If God chooses not to do so, do they still believe that he is a healer?

Like the Hebrew boys, they wanted the king to know that he could if he did not deliver them from the furnace. We must believe that there is nothing God cannot do but also understand that he is not required to do it. The fact of God's existence is so conspicuous, both through the creation and through man's conscience, that the Bible calls the atheist a "fool." The Bible never attempts to prove the existence of God; rather, it assumes His existence from the very beginning.

The Bible reveals the nature, character, and work of God. Knowing God is of utmost importance because a false idea about God is idolatry. A good summary definition of God is "the Supreme Being; the Creator and Ruler of all that is; the Self-Existent One who is perfect in power, goodness, and wisdom. "We know certain things to be true of God for one reason: in His mercy, He has condescended to reveal some of His qualities to us. God is Spirit.

God is One, but He exists as three Persons God the Father, God the Son, and God the Holy Spirit. God is infinite and unchanging. God exists everywhere, knows everything, and has all power and authority. Some of God's characteristics are revealed in the Bible: God is just, loving, truthful, and holy. God shows compassion, mercy, and grace. God judges' sins but also offers forgiveness. We cannot understand God apart from His works because what God does flows from who He is.

Here is a list of some of God's past, present, and future works: God created the world; He actively sustains the world. He is executing His eternal plan, which involves the redemption of man from the curse of sin and death; He draws people to Christ; He disciplines His children; and He will judge the world. Think about this; when we meet someone for the first time, we do not meet them, but rather we meet their representative.

We meet whom they want us to believe them to be. Here God wants us to know who he is, and he also wants us to know that we did not choose him, but rather he chooses us. He loved us before we first loved him. Some people, when they read the Bible, are confused as to what the word of God is revealing to us. Someone asked, "could God ever be surprised by anything"? Can humans think or do something that God did not expect? Someone suggested that God was surprised in the garden after Adam and Eve ate the Fruit.

They suggest that because God said Adam, where are you, they believe that this came as a surprise to God. What they fail to realize is that God asked this question not because he no longer knew where Adam was but rather because he wanted Adam to realize that he was in a different place. Never had Adam had to hide or conceal himself from God? Because of Adam's actions, he was acting contrary to his relationship with God. Also, before this disobedient act, Adam had no shame for his nakedness in the Garden.

Even to this day, when we as people do wrong, we also hide and try to escape blame by directing it toward someone or something else. Another instant is some claim that when Jesus was teaching in the Temple in his Hometown of Nazareth, the people rejected him and his message. They believe Jesus left amazed by their unbelief, saying that Jesus what surprised that those who knew him the best could so easily dismiss him. I believe if we would only study the word of God and meditate on his word, we would not so easily be confused as to what the Bible is saying to each of us.

Jesus Christ is God in the flesh. He was 100 percent Human and 100 percent divine. There was nothing that he did not know.

Remember, it was Christ who told Peter that he would deny him three times. It was also Christ who told his disciples that Lazarus was dead, yet he was just sleeping. It was Christ who told Mary that he was the resurrection. His thought is not our thought. People often time say that people died before their time. No death sneaks up on God.

There is absolutely nothing that he does not know. If we honestly believe any of this nonsense, then we must have to confess that he is not and cannot be God. John tells us He came unto his own, and his own received him not. John also tells us that those who will not believe are damned already. We must study the word of God in it. We think we have Salvation.

Light into Pastoring

Pastoring oversees. And I will give you pastors according to mine heart, which shall feed you with knowledge and understanding. The Greek **word episkopos** means overseer. According to the dictionary, a **Pastor** is a **Minister** or a priest in charge of a church. He may also be a person giving spiritual care to a group of believers. On the other hand, **"reverend"** refers to a title given to an ordained Minister who is a member of the clergy.

Okay, here we go. Buckle yourselves in. I would like for you to walk with me through what I have discovered to be the true issues surrounding the topic of "Women Pastors." My prayer in authoring this book is not to tell anyone what they can or cannot do. I am just asking everyone to examine their consciousness to see for themselves what is true. So, I want to begin by first stating that during my research of these topics, much of what I have read brought me to tears.

I had to ask myself, do these individuals who claim that they are believers in the Word of God understand what they are saying? What I mean is that much of what I have read claims that Paul said this, and in fact, what Paul meant was this. Are you serious? The Holy Bible is not Paul's writings. The Bible is the Unadulterated, Infallible, and Unchanging word of God. **Biblical inspiration** is the doctrine in Christian theology that the human authors and editors of the **Bible** were led and influenced by **God** in their writings of the word of **God**.

So, if we believe in the entire writings in the Bible, then we believe in God. If we do not believe in the entire writings in the Bible, then we do not believe in God. In the beginning, was the Word, and the Word was with God, and the Word was God. It is as if John had said, "I want you to consider Jesus in His teaching and deeds. But you will not understand the good news of Jesus in its fullest sense unless you view Him from this point of view.

Flashlight

Jesus is God manifest in the flesh, and His words and deeds are those of the God-Man." And the Word was made flesh and dwelt among us. Now knowing this to be true. We must decide whether to believe or not believe. But keep one thing in mind. Everyone is talking about making Heaven their home. Well, listen to this. Heaven and earth shall pass away: but my words shall not pass away.

Jesus' assertion guarantees the fulfillment of His prophecy. The present universe will come to a cataclysmic end, **but** Jesus' **words will never pass away.** They will have eternal validity. What is true of God's words is equally true of Jesus' words, for He is God. For we wrestle not against flesh and blood, but against principalities, against powers, against the rulers of the darkness of this world, against spiritual wickedness in high places.

Satanic deception will continue to the very end, and false Christ and false prophets will lead people astray. They will even do miracles. So deceptive will be these miracles that even the elect will almost believe their lies. Of themselves, miracles are not proof of divine calling and approval. The final test is the Word of God. Such limits God certainly assigned from the beginning: Thou shalt come up to this; thou shalt not pass it.

And as he assigned the limits, so he assigned the means. It is lawful for thee to acquire knowledge in this way; it is unlawful to seek it in that. And had he, not a right to do so? And would his creation have been perfect without it? "There is a rule for all things; there are in fine fixed and stated limits, on either side of which righteousness cannot be found." On the line of duty alone, we must walk. Here we know that the office of a pastor was created by God. It doesn't matter what we think or how we may feel on this subject.

We are coming dangerously close to blasphemous behavior, thinking we can change what God himself has ordained. We either believe the word of God or we don't. God is not someone with a learning disability that need us to explain what he means. God himself declares that his word is so plain that a fool cannot err. *An elder must be a man whose life cannot be spoken against. He must be faithful to his wife. He must exhibit self-control, live wisely, and have a good reputation.* Churches today are gathering around men instead of the Lord.

The worst thing a pastor can do in the church is to make the church spiritually dependent upon him. The job of a pastor is to point the people to Christ and make them God-dependent, not pastor dependent. Teach God's people how to study and learn the Word of God and apply it to their lives. Teach them to nourish themselves on God's Word. If you should die or if the Lord should move you on to another ministry, your church should not miss a beat because your ministry has been centered around Christ, not you.

Light into The Controversy?

When the topic of Women Pastoring comes to light, there seems to be a great controversy on the subject. When we Preach and Teach the word of God, we must deny ourselves and our opinions. We should take a step back and ask ourselves why we are doing the things that we are doing. It does not matter what the topic is or what are differences may be. The word of God has the answer for every discussion. There is no controversy surrounding Women's Pastoring.

Controversy is a dispute or argument in which people express strong opposing views. It doesn't matter what we think about these issues. What matters is what God says about these issues. Someone once said, "If God said it, I believe it. That settles it."

Contrary to belief, if God said it, that settles it. It does not matter if we believe it. God does not need anyone to co-sign anything he has already declared. So, there is no controversy at all.

We, especially those of us who proclaim to be people of God, need only to stop wavering between two opinions and stand on the word of God. So, turn on your spiritual flashlight, and let us begin to look at what the word of God has to say. Let us see what we find in **1 Timothy 2:11-12**. The language here is straightforward and clear. But does the writer mean what we think he means? And if he does mean it, is this an instruction he intended for universal application, regardless of historical context and circumstances?

This passage is at the heart of the ongoing discussion of the place and role of women in the church. The answer to this question is critical to this discussion. This passage is a difficult one for yet another reason, namely, an emotional one. I am sure I cannot fully grasp the impact this word must have on women. But given that limitation, I can, nonetheless, understand the disappointment and desire women have to serve in this position. This denial can damage one's self-worth and sense of giftedness this restrictive word must evoke.

We are living at a point in history in which women and men are equally recognized as gifted in intellectual ability and communication skills. In such a climate, this prohibition seems particularly difficult to understand and accept. For what is it about gender which militates against the full expression of the Creator's gifts of heart, mind, and spirit? This question has often been answered with the assertion that clearly defined roles for men and women are divinely ordained and that biblical restrictive instruction is evidence of such a universal norm.

That response, however, is problematic. The account of the creation of male and female, which we take as a foundational theological statement of the Creator's design and intention, affirms male and female as equal and complementary. Both are bearers, together, of God's image. Both are given the mandate to have responsible sovereignty over the created order. The creation of the woman is intended to rescue the man from his aloneness and to provide him with a compliment. The creation account of Genesis affirms the woman to be of the same essence as a man ("bone of my bones and flesh of my flesh").

Therefore, the view that God intended the woman for a restricted role in the home, church, and society cannot be grounded in the order of creation. This we know to be true. We must turn on our spiritual flashlight and seek the answer. Where might we find the answer? The answer is in the word of God. We must not lean to our understanding, but search the word of God, understand the word of God, and accept the word of God. So, where do we begin? Let us Begin with the book of Genesis.

It is clear from the words of **Genesis 3:16**. "Your desire will be for your husband, and he will rule over you." This does not announce

God's created design for a male hierarchy. These words announce a cursed existence because of a broken relationship between the human creation and the Creator. A restriction is therefore placed on the woman. Let us also understand that this is not God's divine purpose but an expression of human sin. I will multiply thy sorrows, and multiply those sorrows by other sorrows, and this during conception and pregnancy, and particularly so in parturition or childbearing.

And this curse has fallen in a heavier degree on the woman. Nothing is better attested than this, and yet there is certainly no natural reason it should be so; it is a part of her punishment, and apart from which even God's mercy will not exempt her. It is added further, thy desire shall be to thy husband thou shalt not be able to shun the great pain and peril of child-bearing, for thy desire, thy appetite, shall be to thy husband; and he shall rule over thee, though at their creation both were formed with equal rights, and the woman had as much right to rule as the man. Still, subjection to the will of her husband is just one part of her curse.

The purpose of Christ's redemptive work was to set God's creation free from a portion of the curse of Eden. If the totality of the curse were lifted when Christ died on the cross, everyone born thereafter would not be born in Sin, nor would women have pain in childbirth. Those "in Christ" were free from the bondage of sin and its expression in human relationships. Christ's redemptive plan restored Man and woman's relationship from Woman being seemingly man; s property to Woman being once again man's helpmeet.

In the new humanity created in Christ, the culturally and religiously ingrained view that human beings, based on gender or race or social status, were in some sense inferior could no longer be maintained. In early congregations, Women functioned in prominent positions (Phoebe, Lydia, Euodia, Syntyche, Priscilla,

Junia), designated as ministers or fellow workers, co-laborers in the gospel. The Spirit of God empowered both men and women to be proclaimers of God's redemptive work in Christ.

Women's participation in the edifying presentation of the gospel and vocal prayer in the congregation was a normal part of early church life. We must never forget that the redemptive work of Christ did not cancel the curse and penalty of Man's sin. We must learn to trust God's will for our lives and press thru our desires to do what the word of God does not instruct us to do. The first question one must ask is the same question God asked Adam in the beginning in the garden. God said, "Adam, where are you"?

I believe God is now saying, "Men, where are you"? Men of God, especially Pastors, know that God has brought us out of darkness into his marvelous light. So, we cannot say we do not see what is happening. We all, Male and Female, preach the word of God, Study the word of God, and know the word of God. Yet we choose to sit silently and say nothing. Why won't Men stand up and state the Truth about what God says about Women Pastors? I would only ask every Man a simple question.

Have we become like the first Adam all over again? Adam knew what Eve had done was wrong, yet he chose to join her. As Adam did hide, the time is now for the Men of God to come out of Hiding. God's order in the church is based on three fundamentals that Paul considered to be self-evident. In the 11th chapter of 1 Corinthians, there is a definite order of "headship" in the church: The Father is the Head over Christ, Christ is the Head of the man, and the man is the head of the woman.

In His redemptive ministry, the Son was subject to the Father even though He is equal to the Father. Likewise, the woman is subject to the man even though she is equal to the man in Christ. Keep in mind that Paul was writing about the relationship within the local assembly. God plans that in the home and the local church, men should exercise headship under the authority of Jesus Christ. As the writer of this book, I am not writing these words to debate them with anyone. I am not writing these words to shame anyone.

I am not writing these words to put anyone down or disrespect anyone. But I am asking all that read the words in this book to examine themselves and examine the word of God to see whether they are true. To fully understand these words, a person must believe in God and that God is God. Why is it that when the question is raised about Women Pastors, the First thing most people say is that Women Can Preach? They are quick to speak about the scripture found in the book of Joel, chapter 2. Joel speaks about the outpouring of the Holy Spirit on the day of Pentecost.

This prophecy relates to that mighty effusion of the Holy Spirit that took place after the day of Pentecost. It states, and the Spirit was poured out then upon all flesh, that is, on people of different countries, speaking the languages of all the people of the earth, which intimated that these were the first fruits of the conversion of all the nations of the world. Thus, we have scripture proving this was the fulfillment of this prophecy by Joel. All nations, who preach the Gospel in their tongues, are further proof that the great promise is in the fullest progress to be fulfilled, even in the utmost sense of the words.

Your sons and your daughters shall prophesy: Shall preach, exhort, pray, and instruct to benefit the Church. During the Old Testament era, the Holy Spirit was given only to special people who had special jobs to do, like Moses and the prophets, the judges, and great men like David. But the promise God gave through Joel declared that the Spirit would come upon "all flesh," which includes men and women, young and old, Jew and Gentile. Certainly, the church today needs a new filling of the Spirit of God.

The word prophesy is not to be understood here as implying the knowledge and discovery of future events; but signifies teaching and proclaiming the great truths of God, especially those that concern redemption by Jesus Christ. These words are quoted to show that, under the Gospel dispensation, neither bond nor free, male nor female, is excluded from sharing in the gifts and graces of the Divine Spirit. So, now let us examine these words. Preaching or Prophesying is not Pastoring? Now that We know the definition of Preaching and Prophesying in detail. Pastoring is different.

Chapter 3: Women Pastors

Light into: Is it Biblical?

During my research on this topic, I came across information supporting Women's Pastoring that I want to dissect. I want to show how some have become blind in understanding the word of God. This first passage speaks to how Women can serve in the role of a Pastor. Although I agree with the importance and value of Women in Ministry. But even in their argument, the bases of what they believe is still Faulty. **My rebuttal will be highlighted in red.** Listen to what this person Says.

I know many women who have been recognized as pastors. No one could say that they are not diligent, steadfast, industrious, and concerned about the Church. A great disservice has been done to women throughout history by not elevating and supporting women in roles of leadership. Many believe and have argued that excluding women from church eldership is sexist, discriminatory, and one more example of male dominance.

Are we sure that this is what is being done? I do not believe that anyone who loves people is respectful to God's Word and knows the painful dehumanization that women have suffered (and still suffer) throughout this country would want to discriminate against women."

To this, I say: Women are one of God's greatest gifts to this world. So, in trying to promote Women in ministry, we must not overstep the authority that God has given unto us. We, also of the household of faith, believe in One Lord, One Faith, and One Baptism. We do not and should not believe in multiple opinions. We cannot and should not place people in positions that go directly against the word of God. And I also say to you that you are Peter, and on this Rock, I will build My Church. Will build my Church, my assembly, or a congregation of people who are made partakers of this precious faith?

Our Lord's expression means that neither the plots, stratagems, nor strength of Satan and his angels should ever so far prevail as to destroy the sacred truths in the above confession. The Church was set up by Christ himself. Are we now accusing God of discrimination against Women? Women are a necessity to Man and one of the greatest gifts that God has given the world. But in our haste to promote women, we have overstepped the Scriptures? Before we get in haste to so-called, make some corrections, let us be mindful of what exactly we are doing.

We must keep in mind that the Church is one body but many members. Every part of the body is important. Nevertheless, as an example, after 15 years of being a hand, the hand cannot complain of never being able to take the body somewhere, and now it wants to be a foot so that it can serve the body in another capacity. We are who God has created us to be. It is our responsibility to be the best of who and what he has created us to be. Many have argued about the qualifications, which I will get to later. But what I will say for now is that I do not believe that Women are not qualified to be leaders.

Being qualified does not make it right. One might say that they are doing an excellent job it still does not make it right. Let me ask you this question if you were thirsty and wanted to purchase a can of soda. You put your money in a Coke machine and press the button to receive a Coke, but instead, a Pepsi comes out. You received a soda, but what came out was not right. This means that there is still something wrong with the machine. You can put out a Fire in your home, but this does not make you a firefighter.

<u>First,</u> the loving, nurturing role of a woman is vital to the health of the church in the same way that it is vital to the health of a child.

God has designed the male-female relationship to complement one another; one gender is not better than the other, but we do have distinct roles. Rejecting these God-given differences can lead to disobedience. Obedience is better than sacrifice. It does not serve humanity well for Men to be put down to build Women up. For many years I have heard from Women that a Good Man is hard to find. As a Man, I would agree with this statement. But to agree, one must also know that this statement is born out of the darkness. You see, the concept of this statement is born out of darkness because a Woman cannot find that which she should not be looking for. A Man that finds a Wife finds a good thing.

Second, many misunderstand male leadership as God designed it; it is not a glorified position. It's the position of a servant. A servant is called to protect, lead, and guard the church. We are to serve those God has entrusted to us. If there is a loud noise at home in the dead of night, do we encourage our wives to investigate? I hope not. God has called men to the position of servant leadership and protector.

Third, we see from Genesis 3:16 that God ordained a leadership role for man. However, when men cower back from their leadership responsibilities, women will step in. God does not need our help. He wants us to be obedient. Men must rise to the call of servant leadership. This type of leadership is not domineering or abusive; it is kind, gracious, and humble. Pastors are to serve those in church, not lord over them. God's design is not focused on "better than" or "superior."

Listen to what God says to Man. And unto Adam, He said, because thou hast hearkened unto the voice of thy wife, and hast eaten of the tree, of which I commanded thee, saying, thou shalt not eat of it. Because thou hast hearkened unto the voice of thy wife— "thou wast not deceived, she only gave and counseled thee to eat; this thou shouldst have resisted;" and that he did not is the reason for his condemnation. Here God is saying because you listened to someone other than me, your wife, you have strayed.

The Second Argument that I found is coming from Women who are Pastors. Listen, I discovered how women and men are learning to lead the Church together. It happens every few weeks. But guaranteed, every time it does, I'm caught off-guard. When you are the person preaching from the Bible each Sunday, leading events, organizing meetings, and pastoring people during the week, it's amazingly easy to forget that being a female and a pastor is a very odd and challenging thing for some people.

Did you get that? She knew within her own heart that it was unnatural. What profits a man to gain the whole world and lose his soul?

It's easy to forget the discouraging emails and conversations you had eight or nine years ago that threatened your budding confidence when you were just starting in ministry, the discomfort you used to have at being the only woman at a clergy meeting, the season during which you knew zero other women leading a church. It is easy to forget that you've gotten used to being you and doing what you're called to do, regardless of what some people say.

In their own words, from year 1, they received counsel as to the position of a Pastor. Instead of following sound advice, they chose to follow their desires. So here she states that she is the only Woman at this Clergy meeting. She also adds that she has gotten used to being who she wants to be. God has given us an inner judge called "conscience" that accuses us when we do wrong and approves when we do right.

A Native American Christian compared conscience to an arrowhead in his heart. "If I do wrong, it turns and hurts me until I make it right. But if I keep on doing wrong, the arrowhead keeps turning and wears down the points, so it doesn't hurt anymore." The

Flashlight

Bible calls that a "seared conscience "or an "evil conscience "that no longer functions properly. For years they chose to ignore what the word of God says. When people are no longer ashamed of their sins, their character is just about gone.

But inevitably, the conversation comes. And when it does, it catches me off-guard. Still. Every single time. **<u>Doesn't the Bible Teach Against Women Being Pastors?</u>** The Question" usually comes from churched people. As a church planter, I have yet to receive that question from someone new to faith or new to the church.

Once again, from their own words. It should not be a surprise to them that people who are new to the faith do not question their position as a Pastor because they don't know the word of God. But the people who do question what you are doing know what the Bible says.

While some of these churched people who pose the question are strangers visiting my church for the first time on a Sunday morning or meeting me at an outreach or community event, others who pose the question are friends and ministerial co-workers from other churches local to me people for whom I have profound respect.

The strangers visiting your Church were surprised to see you operating in that position. The others whom you refer to as Friends and co-workers from other churches love you enough to invite you to re-examine what you are doing. Yet you say that you have profound respect for them, but you refuse to hear them.

The choice to receive this question as an opportunity rather than a threat has come with time and practice. Because I know I am not alone in hearing "The Question," I want to share three things I ask myself when I encounter a person challenging my role as a pastor.

3 Things I had to Consider When My Calling as a Woman Pastor was Questioned. 1.

1. Who is the true enemy here?

There is an Enemy—but they are not it. In seminary, I took a class at Reformed Theological Seminary, which does not support women in pastoral leadership. I knew someday I would serve a church in a community with other churches, and I wanted to have a first-hand experience with what my brothers in Christ down the street believed.

Here even in Seminary class, she admits to knowing what the stance was about the position of being a Women Pastor, but she says that she knew one day, meaning no one and nothing would change her mind, not even the word of God.

In class, I found talented young men with a heart for reaching people for Christ and communicating God's Word effectively. I was told by some that it was indeed the first time they had gotten to know a female evangelical pastor. I believe most of these folks are doing God's work. There is a megachurch by me that does not allow women to be pastors. Still, it has amazing ministries to families with special needs children and continually has an impact on youth and young adults in the region. I may never be invited to preach there, but they are not the enemy.

Primarily, the individuals in the class are not going to treat you like a plague. We are all working for the same goal, and that is to share the good news of the Gospel. You also state that some told you that it was the first time many had met a female Pastor. Could it be because you have already stated that you were the only one? You also say that there was a church that might never invite you to preach. Are you saying that because, in your heart, you want to be invited to preach there?

Flashlight

I have a neighbor who goes to a church that supports a strict complementarian view, yet she supported my church by passing out our door hangers to her neighbors, inviting them to my church since it's in our neighborhood, while hers is far away. Again, she is not the enemy.

Who cares about complementarian views? I do know what it is. If you truly have been called by God, his view is all that should matter. Then Peter and the other apostles answered and said, we ought to obey God rather than men. This neighbor passing outdoor hangers is not co-signing your position as a Pastor. They also know that if anyone has a chance to hear the word of God it will be a life-changing event. It is not about you it is about people receiving Christ in their lives.

I have found that it takes a certain Spirit-humbled posture to step into spaces and relationships with people who have questions about what I am doing. I believe spiritual maturity results in becoming explorative rather than defensive, continuing to be whom God has called me to be.

Trust in the LORD with all thine heart; and lean not unto thine own understanding. In all thy ways acknowledge him, and he shall direct thy paths. He is not directing if it is what you want to do. To be humble means to be obedient to the word of God, not going against the word of God.

2. What ideas have they connected in their mind that they are having difficulty separating?

Once you begin to grasp someone's theological formative identity, pinpoint the area of struggle.

Please forget about your theological thoughts and your

ideologies. Believe the word of God. Theology is a theory. It is the study of. What does it profit a person to study God when you do not know God? Get to know the God of your Theology. Paul had not studied God, but when God spoke to him, he knew who he was. Moses had not studied God, but when God called him to the bush, he knew he was standing before God. Let me speak to your theology and ideology.

When the pharaoh returned from trying to destroy the children of Israel, he simply stated that His God is God. This was absent of any theology or ideology. King Nebuchadnezzar, in the 3-chapter verse twenty-five, stated that one of the Men inside the furnace looked like the Son of God. Once again, no theology or ideology. We either know or we do not.

3. What would be most helpful for them to understand?

They simply need to witness the reality of a woman ministering. I was the first woman I heard preach. You or your pastor might be someone else's first. Receive this as an opportunity and a gift.

What I gather from this statement is that she fell in love with her preaching.

Admittedly I have questioned why someone with strong feelings about women in ministry would check out my church's website and still come for a visit, but I've come to see the possibility that it could be a movement of the Spirit. The Holy Spirit does not always work in boxes.

The Spirit of truth—The Spirit, or Holy Ghost, whose essential office is to manifest, vindicate, and apply the truth. The Gospel of Christ it is called because it exposes falsity, removes the error, and teaches the knowledge of the true God. The Holy Spirit cannot deliver two different truths.

Perhaps they are open to exploring the possibility of women in ministry, and some key resources would go a long way in helping them down that path.

We perish for the lack of knowledge. I do not believe that this individual even understands what she is saying. How can she expect people who are new to the Faith or new to ministry to know the word of God? She also cannot see that it is because of this reception from these individuals that are keeping her puffed up.

Light into Biblical Facts

The innocence and harmony of Creation were shattered when Adam and Eve choose to disobey God, with consequences that affect the entire human race. The story of the Fall is Scripture's explanation for the sin and evils that mar society, corrupt personal and international relationships, and doom us to biological and spiritual death. Satan's devious enticement of Eve reminds us that we cannot be forced to sin. But we are vulnerable to temptation.

Satan first misrepresented God's word, then directly denied it, and finally questioned God's motives. Her confidence in God was thus undermined, Eve relied on what seemed pleasurable to her physical senses, and what seemed desirable to her human understanding and sinned. To overcome temptation, we need to know God's Word accurately, trust His judgment completely and obey with the full assurance that what God chooses for us is both right and best.

As Satan launched an attack on Mankind in the beginning, he also launched an attack on the Church that our Lord and Savior have established. Primarily, Adam was guilty of two things. He willfully disobeyed God and he failed to cover his Wife. To be disobedient to God's word will cause profound consequences in our lives. We cannot afford to be ignorant of the word of God and live a life that is not pleasing in his sight. We are created in the image and likeness of God himself. Here is where we can trace the false teachings of these beliefs. The strategy is found in the Third Chapter of Genesis.

First is the Temptation. A temptation is an opportunity to accomplish a good thing in a bad way. It's a good thing to pass a school examination but a bad thing to do it by cheating. It's a good thing to pay your bills but a bad thing to steal the money for the payments. Satan said to Eve: "I can give you something that you need and want. You can have it now and enjoy it, and best of all, there will not be any painful consequences. What an opportunity!"

For what shall it profit a man if he shall gain the whole world and lose his soul?

Women who are serving as Pastor's preaching the word of God and seeing many come to Christ must understand that the word of God is good no matter who is delivering it. All I ask is that you search the scripture to be sure that you are confident beyond any doubt that you were called to operate in the office of a Pastor. Not everyone that saith unto me, Lord, Lord, shall enter the kingdom of heaven; but he that doeth the will of my Father which is in heaven.

Many will say to me in that day, Lord, Lord, have we not prophesied in thy name? and in thy name have cast out devils? And in thy name done many wonderful works? And then will I profess unto them, I never knew you: depart from me, ye that work iniquity. God has given us free will so we can do what we so chose. But as one song says, "If I should die and my soul is lost it is nobody's fault but mine."

Second is: Satan disguised himself.

Satan isn't an originator; he's a clever imitator who disguises his true character. If necessary, he can even masquerade as an angel of light. Satan still works today as the great impersonator. He has produced counterfeit righteousness apart from the righteousness that comes only by faith in the Savior. Satan has false ministers who preach a false gospel, and he has false brothers (and sisters) who oppose the true Gospel. The devil has gathered his counterfeit Christians into false churches that God calls "synagogues of Satan,"; and in these assemblies are Satan's "deep secrets."

Third is; Satan questioned God's Word.

2 Corinthians 11:3 makes it clear that Satan's target was Eve's mind and that his weapon was deception. By questioning what God said, Satan raised doubts in Eve's mind concerning the truthfulness of God's Word and the goodness of God's heart. "Do you mean that you can't eat from every tree?" If God loved you, He would be much more generous. He is holding out on you!" Satan wanted Eve to forget that God had told Adam (who had told her) that they could eat freely of the trees of the Garden.

For their good, there was a prohibition: they didn't dare eat from the forbidden tree in the middle of the Garden. There was only one thing in the beginning that they were not at liberty to do, and again in the Church that Christ established, there is one thing that women are not at liberty to do. Eve's reply showed that she was following Satan's example and altering the very Word of God. You'll see that she omitted the word "freely," added the phrase "nor shall you touch it" and failed to say that God "commanded" them to obey.

Finally, she said, "lest you die," a possibility instead of "You shall surely die," an actuality. So, she took from God's Word, added to God's Word, and changed God's Word, which is a serious offense indeed. She was starting to doubt God's goodness and truthfulness. Eve should have reminded herself of God's Word, believed it, left the serpent, and found her husband. It is when we linger at the place of temptation that we get into trouble, especially when we know what we're thinking is contrary to God's truth. Satan substituted his own lie **(Gen. 3:5)**.

"You will be like God" is a promise that would get anybody's attention. What is "the lie" (singular) that has ruled civilization since the fall of man? It is the belief that men and women can be their god and live for the creation and not the Creator and not suffer any consequences. Believing this, they refuse to submit to God's truth but preferred to believe Satan's lies and follow his diabolical plan for their destruction. When you review the sequence, you can better understand how Satan leads people to the place of disobedience.

Once we start to question God's Word, we are prepared to deny His Word and believe Satan's lies. When our Lord was tempted, He answered Satan's lies with God's truth and three times affirmed, "It is written!" Satan wants to deceive our minds, but we defeat him by using the spiritual weapons God provides. So, when we believe that God is telling us to do something we need to see if it aligns with the word of God. Satan can speak to us as well. Eventually, every believer discovers that the Christian life is a battleground, not a playground, and that we face an enemy who is much stronger than we are apart from the Lord.

As Christians, we face three enemies: the world, the flesh, and the devil. "The world" refers to the system around us that opposes God, which caters to "the lust of the flesh, and the lust of the eyes, and the pride of life". "The flesh" is the old nature that we inherited from Adam, a nature that is opposed to God and can do nothing spiritual to please God. By His death and resurrection, Christ overcame the world. In other words, as believers, we do not fight for victory we fight from victory!

"We are at spiritual war! We must engage in the fight. A truce will never be a remedy. God's will for his saints is not that we merely survive, but that we thrive in total victory. We must be aware of our enemy if we would have this victory. If you think as a believer in Jesus Christ that you are NOT in a spiritual war, then you are deceived. "When you enlist in the army of God the moment you are born again you are in His army forever you become a target!

Satan's abilities

Satan is a strong adversary, and we need the power of God to be able to stand against him. Never underestimate the power of the devil. It is not a coincidence he is being referenced as a lion and a dragon! The Book of Job tells what his power can do to a man's body, home, wealth, and friends. Jesus calls Satan a thief who comes "to steal, kill, and to destroy." Not only is Satan strong, but he is also wise and subtle, and we fight against "the wiles of the devil." Wiles means "cunning, crafty arts, stratagems." The Christian cannot afford to be "ignorant of his devices."

Some men are cunning and crafty and "lie in wait to receive," but behind them is the arch-deceiver, Satan. He masquerades as an angel of light and seeks to blind men's minds to the truth of God's Word. Satan wants to use our external enemy, the world, and our internal enemy, the flesh, to defeat us. His weapons and battle plans are formidable. Now let us hear what God himself says and understand. **And the LORD God said, it is not good that the man should be alone; I will make him a help meet for him.**

There was no such helper among the animals, so God made the first woman and presented her to the man as his wife, companion, and helper. She was God's special love gift to Adam. **The dignity of woman.** The woman was by no means a "lesser creature." The same God who made Adam also made Eve and created her in His image. Both Adam and Eve exercised dominion over Creation. The plain fact is that Adam needed Eve.

Not a single animal God had created could do for Adam what Eve could do. She was a helper "meet [suitable] for him." Helpmeet or Helper? Do not jump to the conclusion that the KJV is wrong in its translation of "help meet" in Genesis 2:18. Helpmeet is not found in the 1828 Webster's Dictionary as a noun, and you won't find it in academic dictionaries online. Isn't it interesting that in the early 1800s, God's Word was used to instruct and teach? Sadly, in our time, the Bible is banished from the classroom. Now we as believers believe that the Bible is the Word of God. Why is she named his help meet?

Putting all this together, the phrase (ezer kenegedo) means "a helper like his opposite." This means that Eve was to be his "other half," like him, but with the opposite attributes. Though Eve is made to be a "suitable [face-to-face] helper" for Adam, she was not made to be a slave. Matthew Henry wrote: "She was not made out of his head to rule over him, nor out of his feet to be trampled upon by him, but out of his side to be equal with him, under his arm to be protected, and near his heart to be beloved." Once again, here we have Humanity questioning the validity of the word of God. We must believe the Bible as the word of God.

And be not conformed to this world: but be ye transformed by the renewing of your mind, that ye may prove what is that good, and acceptable, and perfect, will of God. This scripture goes on to say, For I say, through the grace given unto me, to every man that is among you, not to think of himself more highly than he ought to think; but to think soberly, according as God hath dealt to every man the measure of faith. As we have many members in one body, and all members have not the same office:

So, we, being many, are one body in Christ, and every member is one of another. Having then gifts differing according to the grace that is given to us, whether prophecy, let us prophesy according to the proportion of faith; Or ministry, let us wait on our ministering: or he that teacheth, on teaching; Or he that exhorteth, on exhortation: he that giveth, let him do it with simplicity; he that ruleth, with diligence; he that showeth mercy, with cheerfulness.

Light into God's Word

Finally, I would like to conclude this section by saying that it is my prayer that all who read the words of this book would just examine themselves to be sure. It does not matter what I have to say nor what anyone else has to say, but we must come together and stand together on the word of God. God is not the author of confusion. We all have a responsibility toward one another. It is not about what we can or cannot do but rather whether are we willing to be obedient to the word of God.

Christ himself, although he was God in the Flesh, stated on many occasions that he was here to do the will of his Father. It is not, nor will it ever be, about our will. Once again, I am not authoring this book to tell Women, not to pastors, but I am asking them to search the scripture to be sure of their calling. Therefore, God said in Paul's writings that the Church is a body of baptized believers with many members but one body. The body can have only one head. Anything with two heads is a freak of nature.

I would also ask Men and Women to visit **2 Corinthians 12:9**. In this scripture, Paul writes about a struggle he had wanting to do something God did not call him to do. And lest I be exalted above measure through the abundance of the revelations, there was given to me a thorn in the flesh, the messenger of Satan to buffet me, lest I should be exalted above measure. For this thing, I besought the Lord thrice, that it might depart from me. And He said unto me, my grace is sufficient for thee: for my strength is made perfect in weakness. Most gladly, therefore, will I rather glory in my infirmities, that the power of Christ may rest upon me.

Two messages participated in this painful experience. The thorn in the flesh was Satan's message to Paul, but God had another message for him, a message of grace. God gave Paul a message that stayed with him. The words Paul heard while in heaven, Paul was not permitted to share with us, but he did share the words God gave him on earth. Think about it. It was the adversary who told Eve that she could eat the fruit of the tree that God told them not to eat while in the Garden. It was not God that gave her those instructions.

In the Christian life, we get many of our blessings through transformation, not substitution. Sometimes God does meet the need by substitution, but other times, He meets the need by transformation. He does not remove the affliction, but He gives us His grace so that the affliction works for us and not against us. As Paul prayed about his problem, God gave him a deeper insight into what He was doing. Paul learned that his thorn in the flesh was a gift from God.

What a strange gift! There was only one thing for Paul to do: accept the gift from God and allow God to accomplish His purposes. God wanted to keep Paul from being "exalted above measure," and this was His way of accomplishing it. When Paul accepted his affliction as the gift of God, this made it possible for God's grace to go to work in his life. It was then that God spoke to Paul and assured him of His grace. Whenever you are going through suffering, spend extra time in the Word of God; and you can be sure God will speak to you. He always has a special message for His children when they are afflicted.

God did not give Paul any explanations; instead, He gave him a promise: "My grace is sufficient for thee." We do not live on an explanation; we live on promises. Our feelings change, but God's promises never change. Promises generate faith, and faith strengthens hope. Life is something like a prescription: the individual ingredients might hurt us, but when properly blended, they help us. **The worst sin of all is pride**. A person who is rebelling against God is in worse shape than a person who is submitting to God and enjoying God's grace.

It is a paradox and evidence of the sovereignty of God that God used Satan, the proudest of all beings, to help keep Paul humble. I would like this to be the concluding thoughts that I leave you with concerning Women Pastors. When God gave the authority to Man in the beginning, and he did, therefore nothing happened until Adam ate. Also, notice that Eve's eyes did not open until Adam ate. One must ask themselves that when Jesus Christ came into the world, we know that Christ is God in the flesh.

Scripture supports Women working in ministry, but we must not use the masculine label of Pastor when outlining their role. We as Men should always look to wise Women for advice and counsel before making decisions. Husbands counsel their Wives in the home before making a final decision that affects their lives. Women, as everyone, are a blessing to the Church, and we all have a gift that we can use to support the ministry of the Church. We would not survive nor advance the work of the Church without them. Now if the Bible supported women as Pastors directly through the word of God, listing the character traits that they should and must possess in that position, I would be their greatest supporter.

What I believe has nothing to do with my opinion, male dominance, abuse of authority, or discrimination but everything to do with what the word of God, through his instructions, tells us. Each of our roles in ministry is to complement the whole Body of the Church. One thing we must all agree with that is we all know that times changes, but the Truth and the word of God will never change. Why didn't Christ when choosing the twelve Disciples choose a Woman? For God has the final say.

As a Woman Operating in the office of a Pastor, how can your Husband be your covering if you are over him? How can he be the High Priest of his home if you are over him? Paul knew about that power because he trusted the will of God and depended on the grace of God. That same power can be yours today. May God bless and keep our minds stayed on him.

Chapter 4: Male and Female

Light of Creation

I want to say primarily to the LGBTQ community, it is my prayer that I do not offend anyone with these words. I pray that you will listen with your own heart to come to your conclusion about this matter. I am not professing to be a perfect Man; I, like all others, have flaws and struggle to live according to God's word. But like myself and anyone else, we must find within ourselves that conviction in our hearts to live our lives in a manner to glorify the God we serve and the word of God in which we believe.

All I ask is for everyone to know that I believe in the love that God has for each of us, in that he has given everyone Free Will. Because He loves us so much, He has chosen to let each one of us make our own decisions concerning how we choose to live. Sin is Sin. Sin is not a by-product of God himself. We often say that God created everything, but I will say that there is one thing that God himself did not create. Look at His creation. God summed up his creation by saying that everything was good.

After creation, everything was still good. Look at how good and loving God was to Adam and Eve. God told them that they had dominion over everything and owned everything in the garden except one tree. This is the first positive precept God gave to man, and it is given as a test of obedience and proof of his being in a dependent, probationary state. He needed to know that he must be accountable to him. As God is sovereign, he has a right to give to humanity what commands he thinks proper.

An intelligent being, without a law to regulate their conduct, is an absurdity; this would destroy at once the idea of their dependency and accountableness. Humanity must always recognize God as sovereign and act under his authority, which we cannot do unless we have a rule of conduct. This rule God gives, and it is no matter what kind it is if obedience to it is not beyond the powers of the ones who are to obey. God says: There was a certain fruit-bearing tree; thou shalt not eat of its fruit; but of all the other fruits, and they are all that is necessary, for thee, thou mayest freely, liberally eat.

Had he, not an absolute right to say so? And was not man bound to obey? Thou shalt not only die spiritually by losing the life of God, but from that moment, thou shalt become mortal and shalt continue in a dying state till thou die. This we find accomplished; every moment of man's life may be considered as an act of dying till soul and body are separated. In this command by God, we can still see the love that God has for humanity. He constantly warns us of dangers that we do not see, and not only that but he warns us of things that are dangerous for and to us.

As parents protecting their children, we should know how it feels to see them hurt themselves by disobeying what you have told them. Another thing I want us to keep in mind. Because of the love He has for us, He evicted them from the Garden, where they would not continue to have access to the tree of life. God had no plans for humanity to live eternally in a disobedient state. Let me say again that I am not writing these words to degrade, disrespect, or cause anyone in the LGBTQ to be offended. I am only writing about this subject to defend and protect the word of God.

Anyone in the LGBTQ community who believes in God must believe and understand what I am writing about. Anyone who does not believe in God, I pray that you will after reading these words. God unconditionally loves everyone. Therefore, the dilemma that I face is that it hurts my soul to hear people say that God is OK with homosexual behavior. If God could turn his back on his own Son because of Sin, why would you believe that God is okay with homosexuality?

Flashlight

It is impossible for anyone who lives under the banner of LGBTQ can say that they believe in God. Why do I say that? Think about it, most, if not all, LGBTQ claim that God made a mistake in their Creation. Some go as far as to say that they were created a Male when they believe they should have been a Female or created a Female and believe they should have been a Male. So, if you genuinely believe this, then you also must believe that this is impossible. I am just asking everyone not to put God into things we chose to do that is not of God.

Light Into God Makes No Mistake.

God, as we know him, does not make mistakes. As God, he cannot make mistakes. He is all-knowing, all-powerful, and omnipresent. So, if you believe God created you wrong, you cannot believe in God, who created exactly what he wanted. If you believe you know more than God does, then he no longer is God. How is it even possible for us to tell God what or how to do anything? Job 40:1-2 (NKJV) [1] Moreover, the Lord answered Job, and said: [2] "Shall the one who contends with the Almighty correct Him? He who rebukes God, let him answer it."

God uses language that reflected Job's desire to take God to court and argue his case.

"Will the faultfinder contend with the Almighty? Let him who reproves God answer it."

God presented His case; now He allowed Job to present his case. But Job has no case to present! His first words were, "Behold, I am vile!" which means, "I am insignificant and unworthy. I have no right to debate with God."

Now, Job had to put his hand over his mouth lest he says something he should not say. Until we become silenced before God, He cannot do for us what needs to be done.

If we defend ourselves and argue with God, He cannot work for us and in us to accomplish His plan through us. But Job was not broken and at the place of sincere repentance. He was silent but not yet submissive; so, God continued His address. Job knew he was defeated. There was no way he could argue his case with God. Quoting God's very words, Job humbled himself before the Lord and acknowledged His power and justice in executing His plans.

Then Job admitted that his words had been wrong and that he

Flashlight

had spoken about things he did not understand. Job withdrew his accusations that God was unjust and did not treat him fairly. He realized that whatever God does is right, and man must accept it by faith. Job told God, "I can't answer Your questions! All I can do is confess my pride, humble myself, and repent." Until now, Job's knowledge of God had been indirect and impersonal; but that had changed.

Job had met God personally and seen himself to be but "dust and ashes". "The door of repentance opens into the hall of joy. Who is there that can find someone to counsel with God? Whom can you find to bring a case against God? Whom can you find to overrule God's Sovereign authority? For what if some did not believe? Will their unbelief make the faithfulness of God without effect? Certainly not! Indeed, let God be true but every man is a liar.

For what if they did not believe? This is another objection. But if our unrighteousness highlights the righteousness of God, what shall we say? That God is unjust to inflict His wrath on us? I am speaking in human terms. "What then? Or what follows? If it is admitted that some did not believe, does it not follow that the faithfulness of God in his promises will fail?"

<u>Let God be true</u>. Let God be viewed as true and faithful, whatever consequence may follow. This was a first principle and should be now, that God should be believed to be a God of truth, whatever consequence it might involve. How happy would it be, if all men would regard this as a fixed principle, a matter not to be questioned in their hearts, or debated about, that God is true to his word!

How much doubt and anxiety would it save professing Christians; and how much error would it save among sinners? Amidst all the agitations of the world, all conflicts, debates, and trials, it would be a fixed position, where every man might find rest, and which would do more than all other things to calm the tempests and smooth the agitated waves of human life.

But every man is a liar. Though every man and every other opinion should be false. Of course, this included the apostle and his reasoning; and the expression is one of those which show his magnanimity and greatness of soul. It implies that every opinion that he and all others held-every doctrine which had been defended, should be at once abandoned if it implied that God was false.

It was to be assumed as a first principle in all religion and all reasoning, that if a doctrine implied that God was not faithful, it was of course a false doctrine. This showed his firm conviction that the doctrine which he advanced was strictly by the veracity of the Divine promise. If all men were willing to sacrifice their opinions when they appeared to challenge the veracity of God; they would soon put an end to the boastings of error, to the pride of philosophy, too lofty dictation in religion.

As it is written. To confirm this sentiment. David was overwhelmed with grief; he saw his crime to be awful; he feared the displeasure of God and trembled before him. Yet he held it as a fixed, indisputable principle, that GOD WAS RIGHT. This he never once thought of calling in question. He had sinned against God, God only; and he did not once think of calling in question the fact that God was just all together in reproving him for his sin, and in pronouncing against him the sentence of condemnation.

That thou mightiest be justified. That thou mightiest be regarded as just or right; or, that it may appear that God is just. This does not mean that David had sinned against God for the purpose of justifying him, but that he now clearly saw that his sin had been so directly against him, and so aggravated, that God was right in his sentence of condemnation.

In thy sayings. In what thou hast spoken, that is, in thy sentence of condemnation, in thy words about this offense. It may help us to understand that Nathan, at the command of God, had gone to reprove

David for his crime. God, by the mouth of Nathan, had expressly condemned David for his crime.

And overcome is sometimes used concerning litigations or trials in a court of justice. He that was accused and acquitted, or who was adjudged to be innocent, might be said to overcome or to gain the cause. The expression is used here. As if there were a trial between David and God, God would overcome; that is, would be esteemed pure and righteous in his sentence condemning the crime of David.

When thou art judged, the meaning, as expressed by David, is that God is right and just in condemning men for their sins and that a true penitent, that is, a man placed in the best circumstances to form a proper estimate of God, will see this, though it should condemn himself. The meaning of the expression is that it is to be held as a fixed, unwavering principle, that God is right and true, whatever consequences it may involve, whatever doctrine it may overthrow, or whatever man it may prove to be a liar.

Benjamin L. Yancey

Chapter 5: Same-Gender Relationships

Light Into Same-Gender Relationships

Now concerning Same-gender relationships, I write to you these words. Why is it that Christianity is the only religion that compromises its values? These religions worship God. Judaism, Christianity, and Islam are the three major monotheistic religions. Monotheism means "the belief in only one God." These three religions share the central values of family, charity, and respect for others. The basic belief has gone beyond asking for basic acceptance to parading superiority.

During a cultural tug-of-war, gay activists ask the government to legalize same-sex marriage. Everyone has a right to choose to be with whomever they please. A right to live with whomever they please and a right to be in a relationship with whomever they please. I do not agree that a relationship between a Man and another Man or a Woman and another Woman should be called a Marriage. If the government wants to recognize these relationships, I ask that they give it another name.

We all want God to bless America; it is time that America starts to not only bless but give the respect to God that he deserves. It is particularly important for our society to respect everyone and to welcome those with good hearts. But that does not mean we should compromise on God's design of marriage. We are in the middle of a war! People who walk around in the middle of a war, acting as if there was no war, are called casualties!

And there are people all over the landscape scattered around, ineffective in their Christian lives, neutralized in their Christian witness, paralyzed in their Christian activities, simply because they don't realize they're a casualty. In military strategy, one must never underestimate the strength of the enemy. This struggle involves hand-to-hand combat using trickery, cunning, and strategy. But here is where the analogy with wrestling breaks down, for this spiritual battle is not a power struggle but a truth struggle. For us to analyze and define the nature of our struggles and this is a crucial point to understand.

We must understand where this conflict begins. Our spiritual warfare is not about a struggle of man against man. It is not a political struggle, a social struggle, an economic struggle, or even a religious theological-doctrinal struggle. It is not a struggle between human beings. It is a struggle among human beings. Let me ask you a question: What is the one thing that gives you the most difficulty in life? For most of us, the answer to that question, in one form or another, comes down to one thing: People. You may struggle intensely with a family member, your spouse or child, or a parent.

Or you may have personality conflicts and struggles in your office, church, or neighborhood. But our struggle is not against flesh and blood. The only thing we have to stand on is the truth, besides the Lord Jesus and His Word. When you start believing a lie, it will flip you over, and you will not even realize it. You will end up fighting the wrong thing and not even know that there is a spiritual enemy behind it. There is deceit in the world we live in today. Our great fight is not against our fellowmen. As Christians, what blinds us and causes us to forget what Christian warfare is?

We are not fighting against humanity; we are fighting for humanity. My fight and struggles are that it breaks my heart to see this nation, especially those who call themselves believers, put God in the center of our blatant desire to sin and think that God is okay with our disobedience. I am reminded of a song from the movie

"Color Purple" that says, "God is trying to tell you something." Those of us who know the truth need to sound the alarm.

None of us who believe that we are on our way to heaven should walk around knowing that this lifestyle is not pleasing to God and remain silent. This is an urgent matter, and we must shout as a siren on an emergency vehicle to draw their attention so that we might help them see the truth. As I stated earlier, we are in a spiritual war. In war, the concept is and will always be "no one left behind." We must be concerned about all humanity. We must stand together and boldly on the word of God.

Light into The Lie

As I began to shed light on this subject, I must admit that during my research, it saddens me to think how some can twist and distort the word of God. But as I write, I only ask that we visit the word of God for guidance and knowledge into how he has lovingly and creatively established a blueprint for us to live. This creative foreknowledge instructs us as to how we should live together in harmony and love toward one another. For me, this is simple; I believe the best way to seek the correct answer to anything is to start at the beginning.

Therefore, it was in the beginning when the adversary changed the word of God to get humanity to go against the design God had for us. And he (the adversary) said unto the woman, Yea, hath God said, Ye, shall not eat of every tree of the garden? Satan's target is our mind, and his weapon is deception. By questioning what God said, Satan raised doubts in Eve's mind concerning the truthfulness of God's Word and the goodness of God's heart. He says, "Do you mean that you can't eat from every tree?"

Here is the setup. "If God loved you, He would be much more generous. He is holding out on you!" Satan wanted Eve to forget that God had told them that they could eat freely from the trees of the garden. But for their good, there was a prohibition that they did not dare eat from the forbidden tree in the middle of the garden. Satan still works today as the great impersonator. He has produced counterfeit righteousness apart from the righteousness that comes only by faith in our Savior.

In defiance of God, humans exchanged God's truth for "the lie. Once we start to question God's Word, we are prepared to deny His Word and believe Satan's lies. Then it is just a short step to believing anything and disobeying God's word. We are so constructed that we must believe something; if we do not believe the truth, then we will eventually believe a lie. So, with this, the work of Satan was finished. The woman was then left to her natural desires and physical appetites.

This is what draws a person over the brink once the barrier of punishment is removed. Why is it that for many people, "Laws" seems restricting? How could anyone believe or suggest that the standards designed to apply to everyone seem cold and impersonal? Some believe that rules are unnecessary. Some even think all an ethical person needs to do, in any situation is simply determine the "loving thing to do." It sounds good. But just how does a person tell what is "loving"?

How can we, fallible as we are, look ahead and determine the results of our choices, and select the course which will lead to our own and others' good? We must also admit that the Bible itself says that love sums up the whole law. Love is at the very foundation of law. Love is at the root of its restrictions; it is at the root of a parent's rules on a child too young to know what is best for them. When we as parents instruct our children to do or not to do something, we most certainly expect them to be obedient to what we are saying.

We instruct them not out of hate but out of our love for them. Think about this; the difference is rather than you and me looking ahead to determine the loving thing to do, God has looked ahead for us! And in his law, he has expressed principles of morality that lead us to what is good. Yes, God does know "the loving thing to do." And we can never separate His Law from His love.

We who are in Christ's need to concentrate on love, rejecting all those sins that distract the lost. Love calls us to clothe ourselves with the Lord Jesus Christ and not think about how to gratify the desires of humanity's sinful nature.

Flashlight

Light into the Debate

I would like to share with you some comments that were given to me concerning this topic. I do not know who made them, nor do I know if they came from other writings. My rebuttal to what they claim is highlighted in **bold**. (let us begin)

At the heart of the claim that the Bible is clear "that homosexuality is forbidden by God" is poor biblical teaching and a cultural bias read into the Bible. The Bible says nothing about "homosexuality" as an innate personality dimension. Sexual orientation was not understood in biblical times. There are references in the Bible to same-gender sexual behavior, and all of them are undeniably negative. But what is condemned in these passages is the violence, idolatry, and exploitation related to the behavior, not the same-gender nature of the behavior.

Thou shalt not lie with mankind, as with womankind: it is an abomination. This passage, to me, is Crystal Clear. It is precise and straight to the point. It also has nothing to do with violence, idolatry, or anything else. God meant exactly what is stated in this passage "Thou shalt not" is clear. If a man also lies with mankind, as he lieth with a woman, both have committed an abomination. We see here that God has given humanity something unusual.

First, He says to man, "Be fruitful, and multiply, and replenish the earth." We will hear Him repeat that when He creates woman. God seems to be the One who introduced the subject of sex. It is quite interesting that our generation thinks that they have made a discovery, that they are the Columbus that discovered sex. God mentions it here at the very beginning.

Also, they mention Sexual orientation was not understood in Biblical times. Sexual orientation is about who you are attracted to and want to have relationships with. Sexual orientations include gay, lesbian, straight, bisexual, and asexual. Sexual orientation is

different from gender and gender identity. Sexual orientation is about whom you are attracted to and who you feel drawn to romantically, emotionally, and sexually. If God instructs us in the eighteen chapters of Leviticus whom we are not to have relationships with, does not that suggest that God does indeed know about our inward desires?

There was no word in Hebrew, Aramaic, or Greek for "homosexual" or "homosexuality." These words were invented near the end of the 19th century when psychoanalysts began to discover and understand sexuality as an essential part of the human personality in all its diversity. Consequently, it cannot be claimed that the Bible says anything at all about it. The writers of the Bible had neither the understanding of it nor the language for it.

So, this person is really confused. You cannot say that the writers of the Bible had no understanding of same-gender relationships or that the word gay person was invented in the 19th century when your entire argument is based on what is described as same-gender acts. Also, whoever holds this belief cannot say that they believe in God or the word of God.

For we know that God inspired men to write the Bible, so are you saying that God himself didn't know anything about same-gender relationships? But the same God who inspired these men to write the Bible states that Men shall not lay with mankind as with a woman. Seems to me God knows more than they think.

Sexuality is a wonderful gift from God. It is more than genital behavior. It is the way we embody and expresses ourselves in the world. But we cannot love another person intimately without embodying that love, without using our bodies to love. And that does involve genital behavior. Sexual love is to give and receive pleasure with our most intimate partner. It is a means of deepening and strengthening the intimate union that exists. This can only be healthy and good if our behavior is consistent with who we are and with whom we love and when we are true to our sexuality and orientation.

God created human sexuality himself, and it is intended as a gift. Within the framework of marriage (Gen. 2), sexual expression is a joyful affirmation of a couple's intimacy, and God Himself blesses every pleasure. Does he hold accountable those who claim to know Him and possess His Word? There are dire consequences to sexual sins, and the judgment is greatest where the light has been the brightest. My friend, God condemns it! In the Old Testament, He condemns it; in the New Testament, He condemns it. "Wherefore God also gave them up to uncleanness through the lusts of their hearts, to dishonor their bodies between themselves.

Sex is God's invention. It is He who created human beings, male and female; He who told the first pair to be fruitful and to multiply. How can a man being with another man or a woman being with another woman be fruitful and multiply? There is absolutely nothing that we can do to change the creative design for procreation. There are four methods that God has used to get humanity into this universe.

One was by direct creation, which produced Adam. A second way was by indirect creation, which produced Eve. The third was by the virgin birth, and this was how Jesus Christ came into the human family. The fourth way is by natural generation, and that is well known in our day.

How do I view God's position on "homosexuality?" I believe lesbian, gay, and bisexual people to be a part of God's wondrous creation, created to be just who they are and completely loved and treasured by God. I believe God does not intend for anyone to be alone but to live in companionship. And God expects healthy loving relationships to include sexual love. The Bible does not say this, of course. But neither does it deny it.

Benjamin L. Yancey

I believe this to be true not only because of the Bible's emphasis on the goodness of God's creation and the supreme value of love but because of the greater understanding of human nature that we have available to us today. I do not believe that God intends us to live in the small world of ancient biblical culture but rather in God's larger evolving world informed by science, reason, and experience.

Humanity has always struggled to define love and is constantly redefining it, but God's definition is clear and will never change. "God is love." Love is not sex, but couples express their love physically in sexual ways, including intercourse. Sexual Intercourse Definition. Sexual intercourse, or copulation, is the deposition of sperm into a female via a male intromittent organ. But sex has a specific and wonderful function in the human experience. While pleasurable and exciting, sex is designed as a bonding experience: an expression of union and oneness to be known by one man and one woman who commit themselves to each other for life.

Light Into Marriage Created By God

Let me add a scripture here for you to examine. And He said to them, "Whose image and inscription is this?" They said to Him, "Caesar's." And He said to them, "Render therefore to Caesar the things that are Caesar's, and to God the things that are God's." Render, therefore, unto Caesar; the conclusion is drawn from their premises. You acknowledge this to be Caesar's coin; this coin is current in your land; the currency of this coin shows the country to be under the Roman government, and your acknowledgment that it is Caesar's proves you have submitted.

Do not, therefore, be unjust; but render to Caesar the things which you acknowledge to be his; at the same time, be not impious, but render unto God the things which belong to God. This answer is full of consummate wisdom. It establishes the limits, regulates the rights, and distinguishes the authority of the two empires of heaven and earth. The image of princes stamped on their coin denotes that temporal things belong all to their government.

The image of God stamped on the soul denotes that all its faculties and powers belong to God and should be employed in his service. But while the earth is agitated and distracted with the question of political rights and wrongs, the reader will naturally ask, what does a man owe to Caesar? —to the civil government under which he lives? Our Lord has answered the question—That which IS Caesar's. But what is it that is Caesar's? 1. Honor. 2. Obedience. And 3. Tribute.

The civil government under which a man lives and by which he is protected demands his honor and reverence. The laws which are made for the suppression of evildoers and the maintenance of good order, which are calculated to promote the benefit of the whole, and the comfort of the individual, should be religiously obeyed. The government that charges itself with the support and defense of the whole should have its unavoidable expenses, however great, repaid by the people on whose behalf they are incurred; therefore, we should pay tribute.

But remember, if Caesar should intrude into the things of God, coin a new creed, or broach a new Gospel, and affect to rule the conscience, while he rules the state, in these things Caesar is not to be obeyed; he is taking the things of God, and he must not get them. Christians must honor and obey rulers. It is taught that Christians have dual citizenship in heaven and on earth. We must respect our earthly rulers (or elected leaders), obey the law, pay taxes, and pray for all who are in authority. Christians must honor and obey God.

The best citizen honors his country because he worships God. Man bears God's image and owes God his all. Caesar's image was on the coin; God's image was on the man. Sin has marred that image, but through Jesus Christ, it can be restored. The relationship between religion and government is personal and individual. It is wrong for the government to control the church or for the church to control the government. From the very beginning, when God created mankind, he instructed them to be fruitful and multiply. This most certainly cannot be accomplished when it goes against our true nature.

For us, as a people, to live according to our purpose, we must fight against our desires to live contrary to the word of God. Respect does not mean compromise. Yes, every person deserves respect, but that doesn't mean we should disembowel ourselves of our moral convictions. What happened to respect for God? Again, here are the comments shared with me. My rebuttal will be highlighted in **bold**.

Regarding marriage, it is important to remember that the Bible was written in a patriarchal culture that assumed men were in control and women were subject to them. Marriage was not an equal partnership but a matter of a man owning a woman or a woman as property. Women provided men companionship, children, and labor. Certainly, love between the man and woman could develop, but love was not the basis of marriage. Consequently, the biblical concept of marriage is not appropriate today. We no longer accept the inferiority of women and the superiority of men. We no longer accept marriage to be a property transaction.

Marriage is a gift from God. God gave marriage as a gift to Adam and Eve. They were created perfectly for each other. Marriage was not just for convenience, nor was it brought about by any culture. God designed marriage. The marriage relationship that God designed has three basic aspects: (1) the man leaves his parents and, in a public act, promises himself to his wife; (2) the man and woman are joined together by taking responsibility for each other's welfare and by loving the mate above all others; (3) the two become one flesh in the intimacy and commitment of sexual union that is reserved for marriage. Strong marriages include all three of these aspects.

The concept of marriage has evolved throughout history. Today, we understand it to be a voluntary spiritual relationship based on love, respect, mutuality, and commitment. What matters is the quality of the relationship, not the gender of the persons involved. And marriage was created not by religious ceremonies or civil government. It's created by the persons involved who make their commitments to one another, whether or not there is a religious ceremony to celebrate the marriage or a marriage license to legalize it.

The marriage two people make together in private is real and valid and should be honored as such. I hasten to add that marriage should never be understood as a requirement for two people in a relationship. Intimate relationships must not always create a marriage commitment. Marriage is a lifelong commitment that not everyone is willing to make or should make. Being single in an intimate relationship is an honorable choice.

Benjamin L. Yancey

It is not good that the man should be alone. I will make him a help meet for him; a help, a counterpart of himself, one formed from him, and a perfect resemblance of his person. And this implies that the woman was to be a perfect resemblance to the man, possessing neither inferiority nor superiority but being in all things like and equal to himself. As the man was created a social creature, it was not proper that he should be alone; for to be alone, without a matrimonial companion, was not good.

God's pattern for marriage was, as the traditional marriage ceremony states, "Marriage was born in the loving heart of God for the blessing and benefit of mankind." No matter what the courts may decree or society may permit, when it comes to marriage, God has the first word, and He will have the last word. Let me say again that I am not writing these words to degrade, disrespect, or cause anyone in the LGBTQ to be offended.

I am only writing about this subject to defend and protect the word of God. Anyone in the LGBTQ community who believes in God must believe and understand what I am writing about. Anyone who does not believe in God, I pray that you will after reading these words. God unconditionally loves everyone. Therefore, the dilemma that I face is that it hurts my soul to hear people say that God is okay with same-gender relationship behavior.

I am just asking everyone not to put God into things we choose to do that is not of God. Secondly, it is impossible for anyone who calls themselves a gay person to even believe in God. Why do I say that? Think about it; some LGBTQ people claim that they were created a Male when they believe they should have been a Female or created a Female and believe they should have been a Male. So, if you honestly believe this, then you also must believe that this is impossible.

When you look at what is defined as LGBTQ, you will find that (L) lesbian is a woman who is attracted to another woman. (G) gay

Flashlight

is usually referred to as a man attracted to a man.(B) bisexual indicates an attraction to both genders. (T) transgender is a term that indicates a person's gender identity is different from the gender associated with their birth. (Q) Queer is often considered an umbrella term for anyone who is non-heterosexual.

Transexual refers to people who have undergone a sex change procedure. Some people may still use transsexual to refer to a person with a different gender identity than the sex a doctor assigned them at birth. A doctor did not assign gender; God did. How can any human tell God that he is wrong? This is calling God a liar.

Light Into The Answer God's Solution

But if we walk in the light, as he is in the light, we have fellowship one with another, and the blood of Jesus Christ his Son cleanseth us from all sin. If we say that we have not sinned, we make him a liar, and his word is not in us. Let me add a footnote here. **Sin is sin**, but one can find that there is a grave difference when you examine the ugliness of sin. I often tell people that when we look at sin, we must remember that God hates sin. Now knowing this, I would like everyone to know that if you have **sin in you**, you are okay because the word of God tells us that we Sin daily.

If we say that we have no sin, we deceive ourselves, and the truth is not in us. On the other hand, if you have **Sinned on you**, then you have not accepted Jesus Christ as your personal Savior, and your Sin debt hasn't been settled; therefore, you will make the payment for your Sins. And such were some of you. But you were washed, but you were sanctified, but you were justified in the name of the Lord Jesus and by the Spirit of our God. The exceeding grace of God could recover any such persons from their sins, leaving a deep sense of the sovereign mercy of God.

But ye are washed. Washing is an emblem of purifying. They had been made pure by the Spirit of God. Three words-washed, sanctified, justified-here denote the various agencies of the Holy Spirit by which they had been recovered from sin. **Ye are sanctified**. This denotes the progressive and advancing process of purifying, which succeeds in regeneration in the Christian. Regeneration is the commencement, but the work was advancing, and they were, in fact, under a process of sanctification.

But ye are justified. Your sins are pardoned, and you are accepted as righteous and will be treated as such on account of the merits of the Lord Jesus Christ. We are justified when we believe and when the work of sanctification commences in the soul in the name of the Lord Jesus. That is, by the Lord Jesus, by his authority, appointment, and influence.

All this had been accomplished through the Lord Jesus; that is, in his name, remission of sins had been proclaimed to them, and by his merits, all these favors had been conferred on them. And by the Spirit of our God. The Holy Spirit. All this has been accomplished by his agency on the heart. This verse brings in the whole subject of redemption and states most emphatically the various stages by which a sinner is saved, and by this single passage, we may obtain all the essential knowledge of the plan of Salvation.

All things are lawful unto me. The expression, "all things are lawful," is used by those who palliated certain indulgences or who vindicated the vices here referred to. Paul designed to meet all that could be said on this subject and to show them that these indulgences could not be proper for Christians and could not in any way be defended. We cannot Believe in God and admit that same-gender relationship is, in any case, right, but we must spread the word that the practice cannot be defended in any way or by any of the arguments which had been or could be used.

For this purpose, (1.) Admitting that all things were lawful, yet many things ought not to be indulged in. (2.) Admitting that they were lawful.

Yet, a man ought not to be under the power of any improper indulgence and should abandon any habit when it controls him. (3.) That homosexuality was wrong and against creation's very nature and essence.

This is the first answer to the objection. Anything that does evil- however small and no good, should be abandoned at once. But I will not be brought under the power. It will not subdue me; I will not become the slave of it. Of any. Of any act or habit, no matter what, it is not to be the slave to it, not to be consumed by any practice that might corrupt my mind, fetter my energies, or destroy my freedom as a person and as a Christian. We may observe that this is a good rule to act on. It requires a high order of virtue.

Anyone that have not the courage and firmness enough to act on this rule should doubt whether they have accepted Christ in their life. If they are a voluntary slave to a same-gender relationship, how can they be a Christian? If they do not love Jesus Christ, our Saviour, enough to break off from what the word of God explicitly declares is wrong, how could any say that they love the Lord, our self-denying Redeemer?

When we realize that there is nothing that God cannot do, we will seek him and him alone for the help and guidance that we need. We need to cast our cares on him, for he cares for us. He asked Abraham, " is there anything too hard for me." If God can bless Abraham to become a father at the age of one hundred years old and Sarah to give birth at the age of ninety, what is it that God cannot do? Trust in the Lord with all our might and lean not to our own understanding. Let us follow the light of the word of God. Jesus Christ is the light of the world.

Chapter 6: God's Flashlight

Flashlight: Let our light shine.

Let your light so shine before men, that they may see your good works, and glorify your Father which is in heaven. In the same way," that light shines from a stand, Christ's disciples must let their light shine before others by letting their "good deeds shine out for all to see so that everyone will praise our heavenly Father." Jesus made it clear that there would be no mistaking the source of a believer's good works. The believer's light shines not for himself but to reflect the light to the Father and so direct people to him.

This little light of mind, I'm going to let it shine. Everywhere I go, I'm going to let it shine. All in my home, I'm going to let it shine. Up and down the road, I'm going to let it shine. As I conclude these writings, let me say that I ask that we look within ourselves to see if we are living a life pleasing to God. Let no one judge you but let each of us examine ourselves. As 2 Timothy says, "study to show thy self-approved unto God as a workman I need not be ashamed but rightly divide the word of truth.

We perish for the lack of knowledge. Also, I am asking those who profess to be believers and even those who do not believe in God to seek a true answer and revelation from God himself through his word and his word only. Please do not be led astray by what someone has to say. Search the scripture for yourself. One thing I often ask people whom I witness is that "if there is a Heaven, would not you rather live your life so when this life is over, and you find out that there is, and you made it? Rather than living any kind of way and finding out that there is, and you don't"?

It is a wonderful life. It is not easy to be a dedicated Christian. Our society is not a friend to God or God's people. Whether we like it or not, there is a conflict between us and the world. Why? Because we are different from the world and we have different attitudes. In the Beatitudes, we find that they represent an outlook radically different from that of the world. The world praises pride, not humility. The world endorses sin, especially if you "get away with it." The world is at war with God, while God is seeking to reconcile non-believers and make them His children.

We must expect to be persecuted if we are living as God wants us to live. But we must be sure that our suffering is not due to our foolishness or disobedience. When next you dwell in imagination upon the delights of some favorite sin, think of its effects as you behold them here! See its fearful effects in the garden of Gethsemane, and desire, by the help of God, deeply to hate and to forsake that enemy, to ransom sinners from whom the Redeemer prayed, agonized, and bled. Say to yourselves he did it for me.

One of the tragic things of the moment is we fail to see how Christ's heart was broken because of our lost condition. He bled and died for our eternal liberty. He said, "...I come that they might have life and that they might have it more abundantly". He loved a lost world so much that He went to the very depths of hell itself to offer it Salvation. Let me ask you a question. Have you rejected Him? Have you spurned Him? Are you ungrateful for what He did for you?

Flashlight into The Remedy

Our example is that of Christ Saying, Father, if thou be willing, remove this cup from me: nevertheless, not my will, but thine, be done. This is the Key to understanding humanity's problems. Until we can relinquish our will to the will of God, we will continue to sink into sin. Until we place the word of God in our hearts, we will continue to walk in darkness. He came that we might have life. For us to have this life that He is offering to us, we also need His light. The light of his word will lead us to this truth. Jesus is the light that lights everyone who comes into this world.

We must look within our hearts and visit the garden of Gethsemane. Stand in the hush of Gethsemane and listen. Do you hear the sob of His soul? Do you hear the falling drops of blood? Look in the garden bending low in agonizing prayer, the Savior who took upon Himself your humanity and mine. He prayed that the cup might be removed. The cup was the cross, and I do not mean the suffering of death. The cup was that He was made sin for us. When our sins were put upon Him, it was repulsive.

I do not know why we think we are so attractive to God. The sin put upon Christ was awful. It was terrible, and for a moment, He rebelled against it. It was in the Garden of Gethsemane, under the shadow of the cross, that the Tempter came to offer the Lord once again the crown without the cross. The Lord, however, had come to do His Father's will, and so He could say, "nevertheless not my will, but thine, be done."

He committed Himself to His Father's will, although bearing your sin and mine was so repulsive to Him. Can we dare to look up to God and say: Deal with me henceforth as Thou wilt. I am of Thy mind. I am Thine. I refuse nothing that pleases Thee. Lead me where Thou wilt.

Two Gardens, Two Choices. Can you see the difference

between the two gardens in the Bible: The Garden of Eden and The Garden of Gethsemane? In the Garden of Eden, Adam's choice to sin brought trouble to all. Adam never would have eaten had he known the consequences to himself and humanity. However, at this point, he did not know what the results of his actions would be. All he had was God's Word and its warning. That is all we have as well.

When we look at how Adam chose to disobey God and the outcome that followed, we must also note that the choice to disobey God still has consequences. We cannot continue in disobedience and expect a different outcome. As it was then and still is today, God hates sin. In the Garden of Gethsemane, a potential explanation for everyone was provided when Jesus died for us. There are similarities, however. In both stories, someone has a decision to make.

This decision would not only affect themselves, but it would also change the lives of the ones around them. In the Garden of Eden, God was allowing the destiny of the entire human race to rest upon a decision that would be made in one night. Adam contemplated the choice of evil versus good. He chose evil and therefore brought the curse of sin and death upon all of humanity.

In the Garden of Gethsemane, Jesus Christ chose to die, reverse the curse of sin, and forever bring life to humans by choosing death for himself. Apostle Paul said, "I died, but yet I live not I but Christ who lives within me," we walk in the gardens of decision every day. The choices we make in these gardens give us time to think about our own decisions. We can either live with a compromise of God's Word in favor of what we think or want, like Adam in the Garden of Eden. Or, when I know that it will cost us dearly, we can take God at His Word as Jesus did in Gethsemane.

We know the temporary pain is worth it because we know that God will see us through. In the first garden, we see the love of God as He prepared a perfect place for Adam and Eve to live. God created a life for us to be easy and good. But because of sin, we now see the wrath of God as He judged their sin and disobedience. In the second garden, we see the love of God as He suffered and prepared to die to satisfy His requirement for the atonement of sin. And we see God's wrath as He prepared to lay all our sins on Jesus.

Please hear me when I say to you I thank God that Jesus Christ became sin for us. When Jesus Christ became Sin, God turned his back on him because God hates sin. If God would turn his back on his own Son who bore our Sins, you cannot believe that he is pleased with our Sins, let alone choosing to live in sin. These two gardens have taught me two particularly important lessons that have changed how I view suffering in my own life. The flashlight of his word reminds me that my Lord and Savior know about suffering. He knows because his entire earthly life was wrapped up in suffering. From what I know, Jesus Christ is the only Human before birth on the Most Wanted List. They wanted to kill him even before he arrived. After He began His ministry, He had no place to call home in the world he created. The very people rejected him He came to save and betrayed by one He chose as His disciples. He suffered an agonizing death on the cross for my sins. Our Lord and Savior know about suffering. God will not put more on you than you can endure. Yet some would disagree.

They believe that He does put more on us than we can manage. Because if we could handle it all on our own, we wouldn't need Him. But because the burden is so heavy, it makes us cry out to Him. And when we cry out to Him, He meets us right there in the place of our pain. And He feels what we feel. He hurts when we hurt. There are many ways we can look at life. I would ask anyone who may feel this way to just stop and think for a moment. We are sinners saved by grace. So, Jesus says, "take up your cross and follow me."

Much of what we carry has nothing to do with anything that God has placed on us. We are responsible for the weight of our cross.

Let us stop blaming God for what we have done. Can we see how wrong we are? Adam blamed God for his mistake in the garden when He said, "that Woman you gave me." Let us stop blaming everyone and anything and start taking responsibility for our actions. The devil did not make us do it. These two gardens also teach me that He loves me. He loved me enough to die for me.

I do not know any other person who would do that. He died for me. He loves me. Suffering has a way of making you forget this one important truth. You can spend a lot of time in sorrow, feeling like God has forgotten about you and does not care. I often tell people that pain, no matter how unpleasant, lets us know that we are still alive. My peace comes from the fact that I know God, but my joy comes from the fact that He knows me. I am held in the palms of His hands. I am never out of His thoughts; he accepts me as a friend, one who loves me, and there is no moment when His eye is off me or he is not thinking of me.

There is unspeakable comfort in knowing that God is constantly taking knowledge of me in love and watching over me for my good. So, I must remember that when I am in sorrow's valley. I would like to encourage everyone not to complain when they believe that you are going through it because they are not going through alone. Jesus promised that he would never leave us nor forsake us. The Garden of Gethsemane and the cross remind me of His care. Both gardens help me see suffering a little differently.

I must somehow fit together in my mind the reality of my suffering with the truth that He loves me. My suffering is real, but So is His love. He loves me. All of this helps prepare my heart for when suffering chooses me. Have you ever stopped to think that when you are going through something, God chose you to go through it? How beautiful is it that God put that on us because he knew that we could handle it? If we were honest with ourselves, we would never know what we could handle or how strong we are if we never went through anything.

So, I want to encourage everyone to be a good soldier and whatever you may be going through, <u>Carry and Conceal</u> it. What God has for me, it is for me. Let us take a stand and tell the Lord our God from this day forth, "not my will but let your will be done in my life. We must choose to make a change in our lives. We cannot live a life pretending to love God. He says you love me with your lips, but your heart is far from me.

God says So then, because thou art lukewarm and neither cold nor hot, I will spue thee out of my mouth. Lukewarm water tends to produce sickness in the stomach and an inclination to vomit. The image is intensely strong and denotes deep disgust and loathing at the indifference which prevailed in the church and humanity. The idea is that they would be utterly rejected and cast off.

A threat of which there has been abundant fulfillment in subsequent times. If we are to be found in the same condition, and all lukewarm professing Christians have a special reason to dread the indignation of the Saviour. Think about that for a minute; when you spit, you care less about how it comes out, where it goes, or even how or where it lands. Whatever it is, you just want it as far away from you as possible.

God wants us to be Hot or Cold. One hundred percent against him or one hundred percent for him. Let us choose whom we will serve. Search the scripture in it you will think you have Salvation. Let us walk in the light as he is in the light so that we may live a life pleasing unto the Father who is in heaven. Let us also strive to live in harmony and unity to uplift everyone we meet. May God bless each one of you.

Chapter 7: Sins

Various Sins

I would like to share with you a list of various Sins. I pray that we all would examine our hearts and pray to God that he may give us the strength to eliminate any Sin that may have a stronghold in our lives. We all have Sinned and come short of the glory of God. But we do not have to continue living under the control and bondage of Sin. Romans 12:2 (KJV) 2 And be not conformed to this world: but be ye transformed by the renewing of your mind, that ye may prove what is that good, and acceptable, and perfect, will of God.

1. Disobedience - Genesis 3:6
2. Drunkenness – Genesis 9:21
3. Self-worship – Genesis 11: 1-9
4. Sodomy – Genesis 19; Romans 1:24-32
5. Incest – Genesis 19: 33-38
6. Lying – Genesis 26:7-8
7. Deceit – Genesis 27: 11-15
8. Hatred – Genesis 27:41
9. Plotting Murder – Genesis 37:18-22
10. Idolatry – Exodus 32
11. Murmuring – Numbers 14:29
12. Breaking the Sabbath Numbers 15: 32-36
13. Rebellion – Numbers 16
14. Covetousness – Joshua 7
15. Comprise – Judges 2:1-3
16. Taking Bribes – 1 Samuel 8:3
17. Pride – 1 Samuel 14: 12-14
18. Jealousy – 1 Samuel 18:8-12
19. Adultery – 2 Samuel 11:4, 27
20. Rape – 2 Samuel 13:14

21. Despising God's Word – 2 Chronicles 36:16
22. Self Will – Ezekiel 28:17
23. Attributing to Satan the work of the Holy Spirit – Matthew 12: 24-32
24. Teaching False Doctrine Matthew 16:6
25. Lack of Mercy – Matthew 18:23-35
26. Hypocrisy – Matthew 23
27. Denying Christ – Matthew 26:69-75
28. Polluting the house of God – John 2:14-16
29. Crucifying Christ – Acts 2:23
30. Blasphemy – Acts 12:20-23
31. Unthankful Ness – Romans 1:21
32. Boasting – Romans 1:30
33. Disobeying Parents – Romans 1:30
34. Lacking Natural Affection – Romans 1:31
35. Living in the Flesh – Galatians 3:3

5 Consequences of Sin

1. It brought immediate judgment upon Satan – Revelation 12:7
2. It will doom Satan forever in hell – Matthew 25:41; Revelation 20:10
3. It brought physical death upon Man – Genesis 5:5; Psalms 90:10
4. It brought spiritual death upon Man Matthew 7:23; 25:41; Revelation 2:11; 20:6.
5. It brought disorder and pain to nature – Genesis 3:18; Romans 8:19-22

7 Losses When a Christian Sins

1. The loss of light – 1 John 1:6
2. The loss of joy – Psalms 51:12; John 15:11; Galatians 5:22; 1 John 1:4
3. The loss of righteousness – 1 John 3:4-10
4. The loss of love – 1 John 2:5, 15-17; 4:12
5. The loss of fellowship – 1 John 1:3, 6-7
6. The loss of confidence – 1 John 3:19-22
7. The possible loss of health and even life – 1 Corinthians 11:30

Study to show ourselves approved unto God a workman need not be ashamed but rightly diving the word of truth. Let the word of God be a lamp unto our feet and a light along our path. Let us also walk in the light, for we know that Jesus is the light. Finally, I want to encourage everyone to let our light shine so they might see our good works and glorify the Father in heaven. Seek God that he and he alone may guide you into his marvelous light.

Scripture References:

Light:
Matthew 5: 14-162

Division:
Matthew 22: 37-39
Luke 6:45

Women Pastors:
1 Timothy 2: 11-12
Genesis 3:16
Joel 2: 28-30
Acts 2: 16-21

Pastoring:
Jeremiah 3:15
John 1:1-3
John 1:14
Mark 13:31
Ephesians 6:12

Is it Biblical:
Matthew 16:18
Genesis 3:17
Acts 5:29
Proverbs 3:5-6

Biblical Facts:
Romans 12:2
Romans 12:3-8
Corinthians 12: 7-9

Love of God:
Genesis 2:16-17
Romans 3:3-
Psalms 51:4

The Lie:
Genesis 3:16

Debate:
Leviticus 18:22
Leviticus 20:13

Marriage created by God:
Matthew 20: 20-21

God's Solution
1 John 1:7
1 John 1:10
1 Corinthians 6:11
Hebrew 10:22

Let our light shine:
Matthew 5:16
2 Timothy 2:15

The Remedy:

Benjamin L. Yancey

Mark 8:36   Luke 22:42

Matthew 7:21-23   Revelations 3:16

www.ingramcontent.com/pod-product-compliance
Lightning Source LLC
Chambersburg PA
CBHW050730010526
44107CB00009B/796